A Viceroy's Vin[

Sir Henry Sidney's Memoir of Service in Ireland
1556–1578

IRISH NARRATIVES

IRISH NARRATIVES
Series edited by David Fitzpatrick

Personal narratives of past lives are essential for understanding any field of history. They provide unrivalled insight into the day-to-day consequences of political, social, economic or cultural relationships. Memoirs, diaries and personal letters, whether by public figures or obscure witnesses of historical events, will often captivate the general reader as well as engrossing the specialist. Yet the vast majority of such narratives are preserved only among the manuscripts or rarities in libraries and archives scattered over the globe. The aim of this series of brief yet scholarly editions is to make available a wide range of narratives concerning Ireland and the Irish over the last four centuries. All documents, or sets of documents, are edited and introduced by specialist scholars, who guide the reader through the world in which the text was created.

Other titles in the series:

Andrew Bryson's Ordeal: An Epilogue to the 1798 Rebellion, ed. by Michael Durey

Henry Stratford Persse's Letters from Galway to America, 1821–1832, ed. by James L. Pethica and James C. Roy

A Redemptorist Missionary in Ireland, 1851–1854: Memoirs by Joseph Prost, C.Ss.R. translated and ed. by Emmet Larkin and Herman Freudenberger

Frank Henderson's Easter Rising: Recollections of a Dublin Volunteer, ed. by Michael Hopkinson

A Patriot Priest: The Life of Father James Coigly, 1761–1798, ed. by Dáire Keogh

'My Darling Danny': Letters from Mary O'Connell to Her Son Daniel, 1830–1832, ed. by Erin I. Bishop

The Rebel in his Family: Selected Papers of William Smith O'Brien, ed. by Richard and Marianne Davis

The Reynolds Letters: An Irish Emigrant Family in Late Victorian Manchester, ed. by Lawrence W. McBride

A Policeman's Ireland: Recollections of Samuel Waters, RIC, ed. by Stephen Ball

'The Misfit Soldier': Edward Casey's War Story, 1914–1918, ed. by Joanna Bourke

Alfred Webb: The Autobiography of a Quaker Nationalist, ed. by Marie-Louise Legg

Pádraig Ó Fathaigh's War of Independence: Recollections of a Galway Gaelic Leaguer, ed. by Timothy G. McMahon

An Englishwoman in Belfast: Rosamond Stephen's Record of the Great War, ed. by Oonagh Walsh

'As I was among the Captives': Joseph Campbell's Prison Diary, 1922–1923, ed. by Eiléan Ní Chuilleanáin

Forthcoming titles:

British Intelligence in Ireland, 1920–21: The Final Reports, ed. by Peter Hart

Scholar Bishop: The Recollections and Diary of Narcissus Marsh, 1693–96, ed. by Raymond Gillespie

Loyalism and Labour in Belfast: The Autobiography of Robert McElborough, 1884–1952, ed. by Emmet O'Connor and Trevor Parkhill

David Fitzpatrick teaches history at Trinity College, Dublin. His books include *Politics and Irish Life, 1913–1921* (1977, reissued 1998), *Oceans of Consolation: Personal Accounts of Irish Migration to Australia* (1995) and *The Two Irelands, 1912–1939* (1998).

A Viceroy's Vindication?
Sir Henry Sidney's Memoir of Service in Ireland
1556–1578

Edited by
Ciaran Brady

CORK UNIVERSITY PRESS

First published in 2002 by
Cork University Press
Cork
Ireland

© Cork University Press 2002

All rights reserved. No part of this book may be reprinted or reproduced or
utilised by any electronic, mechanical or other means, now known or hereafter
invented, including photocopying or recording or otherwise, without either the
prior written permission of the Publishers or a licence permitting restricted
copying in Ireland issued by the Irish Copyright Licensing Agency Ltd, The Irish
Writers' Centre, 19 Parnell Square, Dublin 1.

British Library Cataloguing in Publication Data
A CIP catalogue record for this book is available from the British Library.
ISBN 1 85918 180 5

Typesetting by Red Barn Publishing, Skeagh, Skibbereen, Co. Cork
Printed in Ireland by ColourBooks, Baldoyle, Co. Dublin

Contents

Acknowledgements vi

Introduction 1
Editorial Note 38

Sir Henry Sidney's Memoir 41

Abbreviations 111
Notes to Introduction 111
Notes to Narrative 115
Bibliography 129
Index 130

Acknowledgements

I wish to thank the *Irish Narratives* series editor, David Fitzpatrick, for inviting me to contribute to the series and for his forbearance during the long time it took me to honour my acceptance. David's meticulous approach to the text may have lightened (but only marginally) the burden which, as usual, I have imposed on my friend and frequent collaborator, Colm Croker. Once more I have brutally invaded the private lives of friends and colleagues, demanding that they read all or part of the Introduction: I wish to thank Patrick Geoghegan, Jim Murray, Mary O'Dowd and Michael Quigley for their helpful and supportive comments.

I am again in great debt to Aoife Nic Réamoinn and to Fiachra and Oisín for the disruption I have routinely caused to family routines, and especially, I fear, to the latter two for monopolising a computer that could have been better put to more entertaining uses.

I am grateful to the Director and Staff of the Public Record Office, London, for permission to edit and publish the manuscript and for the facilities afforded me during the editorial process. I am happy to acknowledge the kind permission of the editors of *A New History of Ireland* and to Ken Nicholls for permission to reproduce the map on pp. 2–3, and the National Portrait Gallery, London, for permission to use the portrait of Sidney on the cover. Versions of the Introduction were presented before several audiences in different formats; but those not credited here will, I hope, understand my anxiety to acknowledge Hiram Morgan, who, as organiser of the seminar on 'Text and Conquest: Political Ideology in Ireland, 1570–1630' held under the auspices of the Center for the History of British Political Thought at the Folger Institute, Washington D.C., in the autumn of 1995, gave me an early opportunity to air my views. I should like to thank the Institute's Director and Staff for the generosity shown to me on that occasion.

Introduction

In the early weeks of 1583 the distinguished Elizabethan administrator and courtier Sir Henry Sidney, then aged fifty-four, embarked upon what was for his time a remarkable literary enterprise. He began to compose an extended personal account of his years of public life. The immediate occasion of this exercise in autobiography was, according to Sidney himself, the realisation that, despite his best hopes and the encouragement of his friends, his efforts to secure some recognition for a lifetime of service in the form of land, title or other signs of royal favour had come to naught, and that his sovereign Queen Elizabeth remained unalterable in her view that Sir Henry had already been sufficiently recompensed for his efforts. Thus disappointed, Sidney decided 'to play a little too boldly in person of mine own herald' and commenced a long and elaborate 'letter' to Secretary of State Sir Francis Walsingham (prospective father-in-law of Sidney's son, Philip) detailing his services in 'the two great and high offices which I have so long and so often wielded' (p. 43) in order to defend his rightful claims.[1]

It was an honourable explanation for such self-heralding. Yet, though Sidney claims to have written it in haste and with 'only such help as my old mother-memory afforded me out of her store', the originating intentions of his enterprise seem rather less simple. The memoir exists not in a hastily dispatched original, as such comments might suggest, but in three surviving drafts, each of them bearing the signs of emendation and addition. Sidney himself reveals that he had prepared an early autograph draft (now lost), and the latest redaction, edited here, is still incomplete, bearing in its corrections, interlineations, marginal notes and concluding additions clear evidence that it was intended as the basis for yet a further draft which has either not survived or was never commenced.[2] Equally dubious as the claim that this was a spontaneous outpouring is the epistolary form in which it is cast. The earliest surviving draft of the memoir is a pure narrative, bereft of any

Names of lordships shown thus : BREIFNE
Names of ruling families shown thus : Joyce

In some areas, e.g. Clanricard, the family name in larger type indicates the overlord

The boundary of the Pale is as defined by a statute of 1488

The other boundaries shown are those of lordships where these can be demarcated; boundaries shown by dashed lines are approximate only

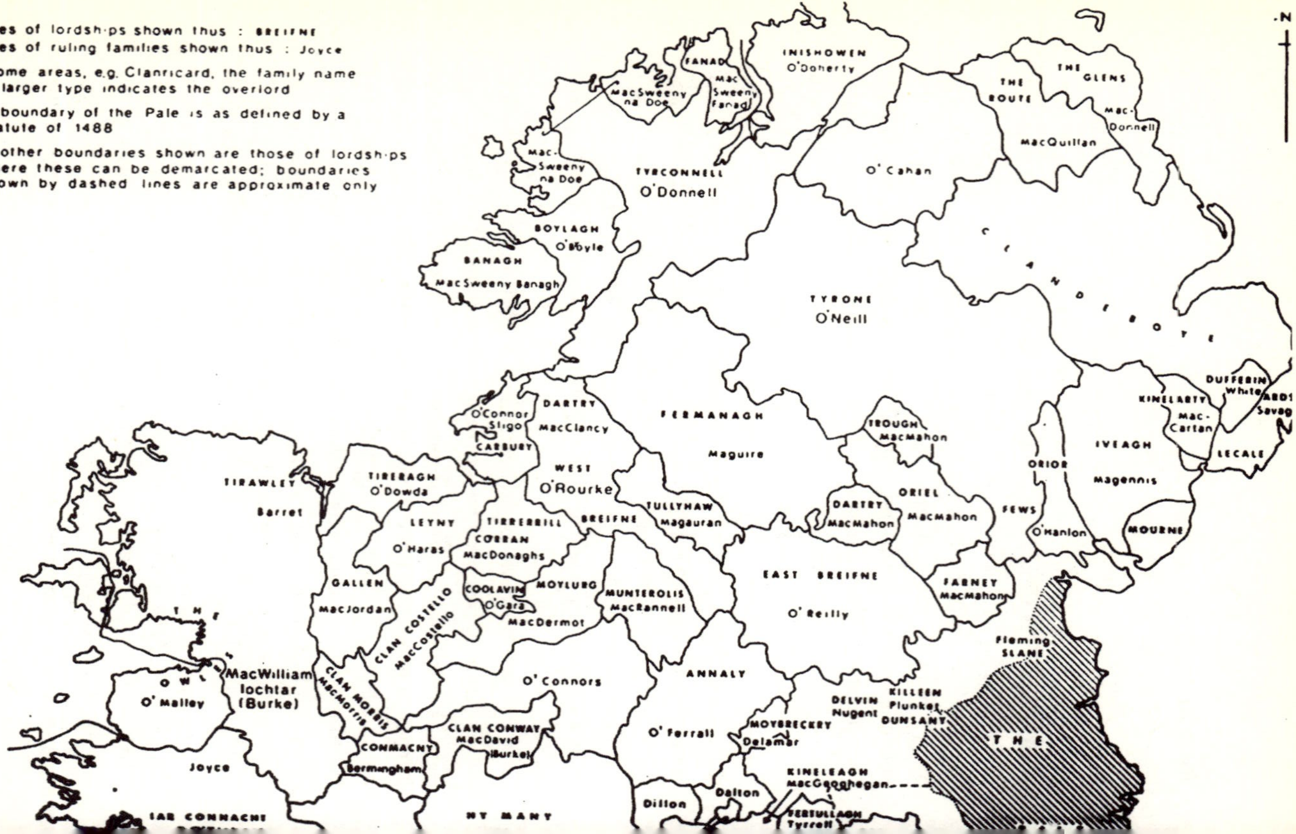

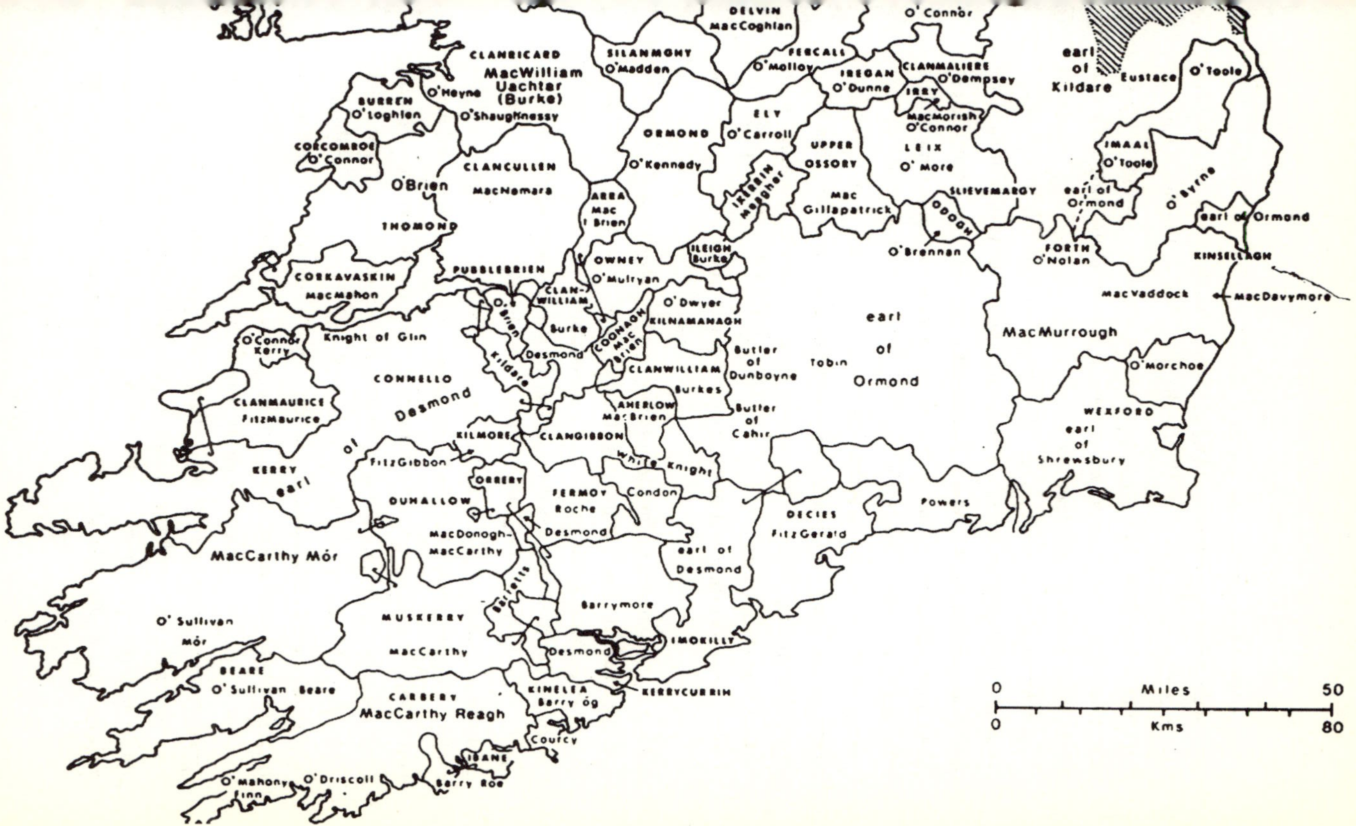

DELVIN
MacCoghlan
O'Connor
CLANRICARD
MacWilliam Uachtar (Burke)
O'Heyne
O'Shaughnessy
SILANMONY
O'Madden
FERCALL
O'Molloy
IREGAN
O'Dunne
CLANMALIERE
O'Dempsey
IRRY
MacMorish O'Connor
earl of Kildare
Eustace
O'Toole
BURREN
O'Loghlen
CORCOMROE
O'Connor
ELY
O'Carroll
ORMOND
O'Kennedy
UPPER OSSORY
Mac Gillapatrick
LEIX
O'More
IMAAL
O'Toole
O'Byrne
CLANCULLEN
MacNamara
O'Brien
THOMOND
ARRA
Mac I Brien
IKERRIN
Meagher
SLIEVEMARGY
ODOGH
O'Brennan
earl of Ormond
earl of Ormond
FORTH
O'Nolan
KINSELLAGH
CORKAVASKIN
MacMahon
PUBBLEBRIEN
OWNEY
O'Mulryan
ILEIGH
Burke
CLAN-WILLIAM
Burke
O'Brien
O'Dwyer
KILNAMANAGH
COONAGH
Mac Brien
macVaddock
MacDavymore
earl of Ormond
Tobin
MacMurrough
O'Connor Kerry
Knight of Glin
Desmond
Kildare
CLANWILLIAM
Burkes
Butler of Dunboyne
O'Morchoe
CONNELLO
earl of Desmond
CLANMAURICE
FitzMaurice
AHERLOW
MacBrien
Butler of Cahir
WEXFORD
earl of Shrewsbury
KILMORE
CLANGIBBON
White Knight
FitzGibbon
KERRY
ORRERY
FERMOY
Roche
Condon
DUHALLOW
DECIES
FitzGerald
Powers
MacDonogh-MacCarthy
Desmond
earl of Desmond
MacCarthy Mór
Barretts
Barrymore
O'Sullivan Mór
MUSKERRY
MacCarthy
Desmond
IMOKILLY
BEARE
O'Sullivan Beare
CARBERY
MacCarthy Reagh
KINELEA
Barry Óg
KERRYCURRIH
Courcy
IBANE
Barry Roe
O'Mahony Finn
O'Driscoll
0 Miles 50
0 Kms 80

address to Walsingham. The latest unfinished epistolary draft is left unsigned. Yet it nonetheless made its way into Walsingham's archive (and was thus included after Walsingham's death in the State Papers, Domestic collection, SP 12) indicating clearly that the Secretary of State must have had good advance notice of its contents long before it was to have been officially received.

The very status of Sidney's text thus poses a difficulty. Not an occasional piece of correspondence which has happily survived, but an elaborately conceived and revised composition which was nevertheless abandoned and left unfinished, the memoir raises complex questions concerning its author's intentions, the context within which it was drafted, and, of course, its actual content, all of which require further investigation. And while many of such problems may lie ultimately beyond resolution, their very existence demands an address to Sidney's work that is at once more curious and more critical than its mere acceptance as an interesting and useful piece of reportage.

A simple comparison of the rudimentary facts of Sidney's life with the account presented in the memoir deepens the text's complexity. In a career stretching from 1550 when (aged twenty-one) he became a Gentleman of the Privy Chamber under Edward VI to his death as President of the Council of the Marches in Wales in 1586, Sidney had been continuously close to the centre of Tudor government. A client of the Duke of Northumberland, the young Sidney was deeply involved in the court politics and external diplomacy of the late Edwardian regime. Deftly surviving the fall of Northumberland and the accession of Mary Tudor in 1553, he served on a major diplomatic mission to Habsburg Spain, helping to conclude the delicate negotiations which issued in the marriage between Queen Mary and King Philip. Dispatched to Ireland in 1556 where he served as Vice-Treasurer, he resigned in 1559 on his appointment as President of the Welsh Council, an office he held without intermission until his death. In the early 1560s he was again immersed in court politics, embroiling himself in the often dubious political and diplomatic schemes of his patron and brother-in-law, the rising royal favourite, Lord Robert Dudley. Sent by Elizabeth on a delicate mission to France in 1562, he sought, without much success, to intervene as peacemaker in the deepening factional struggles of Guise and Condé. Shortly thereafter he was used in Scotland as part of Cecil's energetic campaign to obstruct the claims of Mary, Queen of Scots to be recognised as heir to the Tudor throne. After the failure of another of Dudley's protégés, Sir Nicholas Arnold, as Lord Justice in Ireland, Sidney was once again diverted to Irish affairs, being nominated, through Dudley's influence, as Lord Deputy in 1565. Following a highly active first term, the circumstances of which are detailed in the memoir, Sidney was recalled in 1571. He resumed his duties in Wales, but also spent much time in attendance at court and in service abroad on a number of minor embassies. Following a strenuous campaign, he was again appointed Irish viceroy in 1575, where he governed during three years of mounting controversy. After his recall, under a cloud of allegations that he had 'taken the land to farm', Sidney devoted the bulk of his time and energy to Wales, where, even in his closing years, he was responsible for several administrative innovations and reforms.[3]

Thus in almost thirty-six years of public life Sidney spent most of his time in Wales, much else at court or on diplomatic service abroad, and in all no more than thirteen years in Ireland, during only eight of which he served as Lord Deputy. Yet curiously in a memoir promising at the outset an account of all his achievements, Sidney spends hardly any time at all discussing his career in Wales, refers only in afterthoughts to his diplomatic missions, ignores altogether his experiences as a courtier in Whitehall, and devotes his text almost overwhelmingly to his doings in Ireland in which he had spent hardly more than a third of his public life. This choice of emphasis is odd and, given the sharp contrast between his controversial service in Ireland and his universally acknowledged achievements elsewhere, provokes an obvious question. In seeking, as he claimed, to have some reward for services done, why did Sidney elect, above all, to write about Ireland?

Events in Sidney's life in the two years before his decision to compose the memoir offer a partial, though hardly sufficient, explanation for this peculiar decision. Though initially shadowed by disfavour following his last tour of duty in Ireland, Sidney's credit as an Irish hand began to recover following the outbreak of rebellion in Munster in 1579. In the early 1580s he was once again consulted, most notably by his successor as Lord Deputy, Arthur, Lord Grey de Wilton, as an authoritative source of advice, and by early 1582 several leading figures within the English administration in Ireland had begun to canvass his return to office.[4] The momentum behind such a campaign had grown sufficiently to encourage Sidney himself to advance serious demands—including nobilitation and the grant of the title of Lord Lieutenant—as preconditions to his acceptance of reappointment.[5] But, it seems, he overbid: Elizabeth jibbed, and the campaign on his behalf gradually faded away. Sidney's realisation early in 1583 that the implacable Elizabeth was unwilling to countenance any other favours in compensation for the Irish office rendered his humiliation complete. It is arguable that at that point he might have been stung into asserting a ringing vindication of his Irish years, but, given the character of the text he actually composed, such a speculation is not altogether convincing.[6]

If reward was, in reality, Sidney's principal concern, his adopted strategy was strangely self-defeating; for defiance, as everyone knew, had never been a fruitful means of exciting gratitude in Elizabeth. Had Sidney been primarily concerned with demonstrating his effectiveness as an administrator, he might be expected to have devoted more space in his apologia to his achievements in Wales and to the lessons for Ireland that might be drawn from there. Yet even though such comparisons were becoming common by the time Sidney wrote, and even though his successful career in Wales might have lent authority to his more troubled times in Ireland, this was not the approach Sidney chose to take, preferring instead to restrict his comments on Wales to a few concluding platitudes following his long Irish narrative.[7] Again, had Sidney wished to impress an audience with the extent of his Irish achievements, he might with greater effect have adopted a more precise and more dignified mode of exposition other than a long self-justificatory narrative. The summary listing of revenues gained, lands acquired, rebels defeated, treaties concluded and institutions established: such were the standard itemisations employed by recalled Irish governors, including Sidney himself in 1578, when they sought to justify their term in office.[8] But in abandoning this time-honoured, semi-official form of representation and in electing to provide a detailed narrative account, Sidney had, whether consciously or not, committed himself to a complex literary strategy whose intrinsic compositional imperatives necessarily privileged certain aspects of his career which might have featured less prominently within different forms, and diminished the significance of others which elsewhere would have acquired greater prominence. Thus it is important to ask what lay behind such a compositional preference that, knowingly or otherwise, led him to accept, in regard to his Irish service, a distinct order of interpretative priorities.

By the time Sidney wrote, the composition of memoirs of service was not entirely unprecedented in English court circles. Over the previous century brief accounts of services rendered had occasionally accompanied simple petitions seeking redress or reward by ageing or retiring royal servants, and under Elizabeth there are some signs that such an approach to making suit was becoming formalised. In the early 1570s the diplomat and minor courtier Sir Henry Killigrew attached a brief list of his journeys on behalf the Crown in France, Scotland and elsewhere as part of his suit to be granted a certain manor in Cornwall.[9] And around the time Sidney himself wrote, a predecessor in the Irish viceroyalty, Sir James Croft, had compiled a similar record of his public endeavours in a more general petition for reward.[10] Referring to these and to Sidney's text, the historian Simon Adams has suggested that collectively they may be seen as a symptom of a growing sense within the Elizabethan political elite of a notion of public service independent of and superior to earlier notions of personal clientage.[11] Though the continuing influence of the feudal petition on Sidney and other Elizabethans should not be discounted, the subtle change of address indicated by Adams is perceptible. Yet even within this evolving genre, Sidney's work differs from its immediate Elizabethan precedents in several important ways.

Most obviously, it was by far the longest essay of its kind: Killigrew's 'Journal' ran to less than 1,000 words, Croft's 'Brief Collection' to less than 2,000, whereas Sidney's text is approaching 30,000. In contrast to Sidney's connected narrative, the earlier two are quite disjointed: Killigrew offers a series of annalistic entries hardly more than a sentence long; Croft is slightly more discursive, but his account remains organised around a discrete number of events. Only Sidney provides an elaborately detailed account of his public life. Yet conversely, only Sidney remains so narrow in his focus, concentrating his attention on one segment of his career, his Irish service. Stylistic differences are also marked: where Croft is laconic and Killigrew's style is factual and unadorned, Sidney's carefully revised text is replete with flourishes, Latin tags, colourful anecdotes, even jokes, all of which were contrived to achieve a polished effect. But most importantly, the difference in authorial voice between Sidney's and the other two texts is quite unmistakable. Where Croft is neutral and Killigrew merely the assertive suitor, the dominant mood of what Sidney termed his 'tragical discourse' is at once grandiose and bleak, each phase in the narrative reinforcing the image of a neglected but exemplary royal servant whose best intentions were misrepresented and subverted by malicious interests and whose appropriate epitaph is helpfully supplied by Sidney himself as '*Melius merui*' (p. 81).

Thus while Sidney's text can be identified with a more general Elizabethan tendency to affirm the independent merit of public service, its size and narrative complexity, its singular concentration on one aspect of its author's career and, above all, its grandeur of tone all suggest that in conceiving it Sidney had at once more distinctive and more ambitious models in mind. For a provincial administrator composing a personal account of his military exploits, diplomatic successes and political achievements, one obvious model, of course, was the memoir of the most illustrious provincial governor in Western history, Caesar's *De Bello Gallico*. Like every Tudor schoolboy, Sidney would have been quite familiar with Caesar's commentaries, which were central texts on the grammar school curriculum, and he could certainly have expected his audience to notice some biographical parallels.[12] Moreover Sidney's style, the long undulating sentences sustained by multiple present participles and cascading dependent clauses, so different from the plain clarity of his correspondence, seems like a conscious emulation of Caesarean cadences; and the arresting (though technically inaccurate) triads with which the memoir proper begins—'Three times her Majesty hath sent me her Deputy into Ireland, and in every of the three times I sustained a great and violent rebellion . . . and . . . I returned from each of those three Deputations three thousand pounds worse than I went'—may well have been intended as an allusion to the famous opening of the great gubernatorial journal.[13]

Caesar's standing within Elizabethan literary culture was somewhat ambiguous, he being regarded in some quarters as a tyrannous destroyer of the republic, but in others as the heroic opponent of a corrupt and ineffectual elite. By the time Sidney was writing, however, there is some evidence that educated opinion was shifting steadily in favour of a more positive estimate of the Roman general, one of the signs of this shift being an anonymous play, *Octavia*, written and performed within the Sidney circle some time in the 1570s, in which Caesar is portrayed as having fallen victim to the malice and ambition of false friends. It is possible, then, that Sidney's assumption of the Caesarean toga should be seen, at least in part, as a bold and pointed gesture.[14] Yet important differences in tone between the two texts cannot be ignored. Though Caesar sometimes complains of the malice of the Roman senate and of the wilful misinterpretation of his actions and motives, his is essentially a record of achievement and success, while Sidney's is a dirge of frustration and failure. Caesar's commentaries, moreover, were composed, or at least presented to the public, in the third rather than the first person in a manner that confirmed the authority and objectivity of his voice. Sidney's preference for the familiar and often intimate first person sacrificed such rhetorical strengths and, of course, risked the opposite weaknesses.

There was, however, a more recent Caesarean-style commentary which, while self-consciously adopting several of the characteristics of the classic ur-text, also anticipated Sidney's disappointed and pessimistic tone. In the closing books of his massive *Storia d'Italia* (posthumously published in 1561, translated into French in 1568, and translated from French into English in 1579) Francesco Guicciardini abandoned the lofty voice of the earlier books and began a detailed autobiographical narrative recording his own participation in recent Florentine history, exonerating his conduct and unabashedly laying blame for the misfortunes which befell him in government on the ambition and ill-will of others.[15] Like Caesar, Guicciardini wrote in the third person, and there is no doubt that, in these final books, he deliberately courted association with the great Roman. But as with Sidney, the style is more personal and the narrative detail more coloured. The *Storia* is peopled with distinct individuals: usually good loyal soldiers who are commended and malicious intriguing courtiers who are roundly condemned. Its mood resonates bitterness and disappointment: a warning to all honest souls who would engage in the disinterested service of their prince. Guicciardini's history was well known to Sidney's son Philip, who recommended it warmly to his associates, but it seems likely that Sidney himself would have been made familiar with it shortly before he wrote. It was, after all, translated into English by his former client and declared admirer, Geoffrey Fenton, who dedicated his 1579 text to Sidney's wife, Mary Dudley.[16]

Other, less classical, models for Sidney are also possible. The detailed *Mémoires* of the disappointed French courtier Phillippe de Commines were published in a widely circulated edition in 1545; and while there is no direct evidence that Sidney himself had read them, it seems probable that, like most educated and travelled Englishmen of his time, he would have been aware of their existence and their general content.[17] Finally, attention may be drawn to a later, and perhaps more pertinent, French literary product which may also have encouraged Sidney to launch upon his own ambitious exercise in self-exoneration. This was the lengthy set of memoirs composed by the French soldier and provincial administrator Blaise de Lasseran-Mussencome, seigneur de Monluc (1501–77) in the early 1570s.[18] Some obvious differences separate Monluc, the 'hammer of the Huguenots', from the Protestant governor of Elizabethan Ireland. Yet their careers share remarkable similarities. Like Sidney, Monluc owed his early advancement to the favour of a young king (Henry II) with whom he had been on close personal terms during the prince's minority. Under such patronage he had, like Sidney, pursued a promising diplomatic and military career, mostly outside France. Appointed to the prestigious but troublesome office of governor of Guienne in 1560, Monluc survived a number of attempts to undermine and destroy his government both by local Huguenot forces and by their sympathisers at the court of Henry III, but was at length dismissed in disgrace in 1570 through a series of charges alleging his tyrannical treatment of the king's subjects, his favouritism and his venality. And it was then that he set about the composition of his own 'mémoire justificatif' refuting the allegations made against him, proclaiming his achievements and losses in the service of the Crown, and denouncing the machinations of the great court faction of the Montmorencys who he believed had brought him down. Monluc's apologia gradually worked the desired effect. Circulated in manuscript around the French court in 1571–72, it led, in combination the convulsions of court politics immediately antecedent to the massacre of St Bartholomew's Day, to his rehabilitation and elevation the highest honour of Marshal of France: the dream of the disappointed servitor come true.[19]

Monluc's memoirs, greatly expanded and retitled as his *Commentaries*, did not appear in print until the early 1590s. But in their shorter form they circulated widely within the French court in the early 1570s, and it is perhaps significant that, at the time when they were working their effect for the sidelined provincial governor, two English agents were themselves deeply engaged in the politics of that court. One was the English ambassador to the court of Henry III, Sir Francis Walsingham, to whom Sidney was now addressing his own memoir, while the other was Sidney's own son Philip, shocked observer of the St Bartholomew's Day massacre, whose forthcoming marriage to Walsingham's daughter was ostensibly the occasion of the memoir itself.[20]

To indicate such correspondences is not, of course, to claim influence. The point of these observations is not to argue that Sidney was writing in conscious imitation of some model: perhaps he was, and perhaps not. It is rather to draw attention to the broader cultural context within which he conceived his own work. It is important to be aware, that is, that by the time Sidney began to write his own elaborate account there already existed within the general corpus of memoirs of service a distinct sub-genre (of which he would have been to a greater or lesser degree conscious) which aimed not merely at producing pleas for personal exoneration or reward, but at the more ambitious object of using a formally composed, elaborate narrative whose content and tone were designed to freight the achievements and disappointments of its author with the weight of greater historical significance. It is within this specific literary context that Sidney's more modest English enterprise is best perceived. Yet it is this perspective also which renders Sidney's topical selectivity all the more significant. For even as he was straining by the character of his narrative to invest the status of his public service with a substantial historical import, it is especially remarkable that, unlike the great contemporary memorialists, Sidney chose to write not about his career in its entirety, but confined himself almost exclusively to his years as viceroy of Ireland.

In the light of this extraordinary decision to distil the sum of his claims of public service into a narrative of his years in Ireland, it is somewhat ironic that Sidney's highly individual perception of his Irish experience should have been approached by so many later historians from generalising perspectives so insensitive to its own peculiar status. For while some scholars have read it innocently enough as 'a valuable account of the "the Secret History" of Anglo-Irish politics' and others have simply raided it for apposite phrases and words useful to sustain some predetermined general view of the governor's outlook and intentions, few have been willing to address the memoir as a whole on its own terms.[21] Yet a closer scrutiny of what Sidney actually wrote shows both that the Sidney of so many recent interpretations features only ephemerally, and sometimes not at all, in his own chosen self-representation, while the complex figure that actually emerges from under Sidney's own hand has to be yet fully understood by his interpreters.

Sidney the 'conquistador', for example, the individual who, on the basis of his absorption of the experience of Spanish conquests in the New World, has been credited with the initiation of a 'new departure' of colonisation and conquest in Tudor Irish policy is hardly recognisable in these pages.[22] The narrative yields little overt evidence of the origins of Sidney's views on Ireland, and certainly gives no hint that he had been influenced by the propagandists and apologists of imperial Spain. Equally it offers no support for the view that Sidney regarded his first appointment as a radical break with all that had gone before, but conveys merely the impression that he had been sent to complete a job abandoned by others: that is, the suppression of the Ulster rebel Shane O'Neill.

In regard, moreover, to the specific and frequently made claim that Sidney was from the outset a leading advocate of the innovative policy of widespread and systematic colonisation, the memoir is far from helpful. Like many of his predecessors as governor, Sidney in principle favoured the introduction of small-scale 'colonies of English and other loyal subjects' as a means of developing waste territories and of establishing defences against possible foreign invasions (p. 57). Yet in practice his attitude toward such colonising efforts as were actually attempted was distinctly cool. Though writing in 1583, at a time when plans for the establishment of colonies in Munster were being canvassed in several quarters, Sidney had nothing to offer on the subject, and he was silent too about other projects for the province that had been proposed during his terms in Ireland. It is true that Sidney notes the aborted enterprise of the Champernoune family in the north-east and Sir Thomas Smith's modest experiment in the Ards, but, significantly, only on a loose sheet appended to the latest draft (p. 110). In relation to the ambitious enterprise of the Earl of Essex in Ulster east of the Bann, however, he is unambiguously hostile. Before Essex arrived, Sidney tells us, the town of Carrickfergus had made remarkable progress in its political and commercial relations with the people of the neighbouring Gaelic lordships, and was like 'to have reduced all [those] countries to as good obedience as the English Pale . . . if the violent and intempestyne proceeding of the Earl of Essex and his followers had not been' (p. 60).

Sidney's limited enthusiasm for private colonial adventures is thus clear. But even more revealing is the absence in Sidney's text of any substantial evidence relating to those novel ethnographic and anthropological views concerning the degeneracy and natural inferiority of the native Irish which, according to certain interpretations, was the means by which he justified the new departure of the Elizabethan conquest. In fact Sidney's narrative is strangely lacking the general descriptions of the cultural mores and practices of the native inhabitants which are such a standard feature of Elizabethan travellers' accounts. Thus there is little to be culled here concerning the domestic dwellings, the agricultural techniques, social customs or even the political institutions of the Gaelic lordships, while even the widespread incidence of the Irish system of military exactions and intimidation against which Sidney had railed in the past is hardly adverted to.[23]

It is, of course, true that an unquestioning assumption of cultural superiority underlies Sidney's work: the Irish are an uncivil, rude people, manifestly inferior in their manners and customs to their English neighbours. But more interesting is the fact that, unlike some later Elizabethans, Sidney clearly regards such deficiencies as neither universal nor indelible. Thus while there are some leaders among the Gaelic Irish whom Sidney regards as treacherous or irreconcilable, there are many more concerning whom he is considerably more positive. Sir Barnaby FitzPatrick, the Gaelic Irish lord of Upper Ossory, is clearly a favourite: 'the most sufficient man in council and action for the war that ever I found of that country birth . . . the noble baron, that true civil and loyal subject' (pp. 64, 76). The heir to the Magennis lordship of Iveagh was 'as towardly a young gentleman as ever I knew of the Irishry' (p. 101). Hugh O'Donnell, lord of Tír Conaill and former ally of Sidney's first enemy, Shane O'Neill, is similarly favoured: he is 'the good knight', who, attending upon Sidney 'with great show of courtesy and kindness', continued to honour his promises of allegiance (pp. 48, 88). By contrast, Shane's successor as O'Neill, Turlough Luineach, is unstable and untrustworthy. But significantly these are, for Sidney, defects of personality rather than type, and Sidney is happy to boast that through shrewd diplomacy and through the good influence of his Scottish wife, Agnes Campbell, who is lavishly praised in the narrative as 'a good counsellor . . . a well-wisher to peace, and a reverent speaker of the Queen's majesty', the O'Neill has at length been drawn to a permanent settlement (pp. 75, 83). In similar fashion, the Earl of Thomond is himself foolish and rash, but not beyond redemption, especially when Sidney counterpoised to him two of his kinsmen, 'as well born in blood as he, but my faithful and true servants' (p. 75).

Few other Gaelic Irish figures feature in such detail in Sidney's text. But what is noticeable is the large number of lesser families whose names and locations are mentioned with surprising precision. The index lists over fifty of such dynastic groups who feature as the subjects of the same micro-drama in the text that is repeatedly enacted: that they came in to Sidney as their viceroy, sued for recognition of their status as subjects of the queen, received it, and in gratitude agreed to render handsome revenues and services to the Crown henceforth. The tone of superiority is again unmistakable, but the effectiveness of the process of assimilation is equally clear: 'I found such humbleness in them' Sidney observes of the lords, gentry and commons of Munster, 'and willingness to become English, and accordingly to live under English law, and by the same to be defended, each weaker from his stronger neighbour, as I did ask nothing but it was granted' (p. 85). Sidney here is characteristically condescending. But occasionally he is more generous. 'In truth, Sir,' he writes of the Gaelic inhabitants of south Leinster, 'all these Irish people, albeit their country were not shired, yet lived they as loyally as any people in the shire ground . . . They were rich, and everything plentiful in their country, no waste land, but (as they term it there) it bare corn or horn' (p. 92). Sidney is rarely so enthusiastic. Yet the point is that throughout his narrative the voice adopted is clearly not that of one who regarded the native

Irish as anthropologically inferior, incorrigible and thus so fit for conquest and dispossession. It is rather that of a hard-headed provincial governor who believed that with sufficient shrewdness, toughness and patience he could make the locals come to see the benefit of yielding obedience to the government he represented.

In other respects also, the Sidney of the present text will disappoint some recent interpretations. For those who have suggested that in his general hostility to the old colonial community, the English of Irish birth, he was an early exponent of a hardening exclusivist line typical of the 'new English', he offers little consistent support. Evil figures among the English-Irish certainly feature prominently in the narrative, but they too feature as individuals rather than as representative types. The Earl of Desmond, of course, is an 'arch-traitor' for whom (in a text written while he was still in rebellion) there could be no mercy; and for the Earl of Ormond and his kin, Sidney, as we shall see, has reserved an especially villainous role. But once more Sidney is carefully discriminating. In regard to the lesser nobility and gentry of Munster he is especially complimentary, praising the Lords Barry and Roche for their generosity and civility. Towards the Earl of Kildare (in disgrace and in the Tower of London at the time of writing) he retains a surprisingly respectful tone; the Lord of Louth and other borderers of the Pale, he acknowledges, have done good service; and even the strongly gaelicised MacWilliam Burkes of Mayo are not, for Sidney, beyond reconciliation. But most interesting is Sidney's attitude towards the Earl of Desmond's brother, Sir John. Though Sir John was notorious as the assassin of Henry Davells and the rest of his mission sent to negotiate a truce with Desmond in 1579 and as the ally of the Counter-Reformation militant Nicholas Sanders, Sidney, even in 1583, refuses to endorse a blanket condemnation of this pariah. Instead he depicts Sir John as an intelligent and originally well-meaning figure who would have been capable of restraining his rash brother and preserving peace in Desmond if only he had been sufficiently accredited and rewarded for his good services in the past. But instead the mistrust with which he had been treated and his arrest, against Sidney's advice, along with the earl in 1567, had been fatal: for 'truly . . . this hard dealing with Sir John of Desmond was the origin of James FitzMaurice's rebellion, and consequently of all the evil and mischief in Munster which since . . . has cost the crown of England and that country a hundred thousand pounds' (p. 58).

Sidney is equally discriminating in treating of the heartland of English-Ireland, the Pale. Though in his closing pages he is deeply bitter about the manner in which the Pale community opposed and subverted his 'composition' (a tax commuting all military exactions of the Crown into a fixed annual sum), he is quite precise about the origins of the resistance. It was the rich men of the Pale, not the community as a whole, who duped the poor into believing they shared a common cause. Sidney bluntly attributes malice and even darker ambitions to some of the leadership of the opposition; but towards other prominent figures within the community he is both respectful and, in the case of Sir Lucas Dillon, remarkably warm (pp. 67–8). Overall, however, Sidney's narrative conveys no sense that he regarded the Pale as a whole as enemy territory, or the bulk of its inhabitants as fundamentally hostile to English government, but suggests on the contrary that he continued to view the Pale as the core of English civility in Ireland from which the process of assimilation was to spread.

The persistent differentiation which Sidney makes between individuals good and bad also raises problems for another interpretative frame which historians have imposed on him: Sidney the zealous enforcer of Protestant reform.[24] In relation to the most obnoxious of the troublesome Palesmen, Sidney was ready to apply the term 'papist' as proof of their larger subversive intentions. Yet in the memoir as a whole it is remarkable how little the standard problems of religious practice, conformity and dissent are addressed. The physical decay of the church fabric, the poverty and ignorance of the local clergy, the indifference and hostility of the laity—all the issues which had concerned him during his viceroyalties and were the subject of some of his most trenchant official correspondence—hardly feature at all in his recollections.[25] In contrast too to his roll-call of secular friends and enemies, neither his closest allies among the reforming clergy nor his most serious opponents receive mention. And amazingly, despite the involvement of Spanish and papal forces in the Desmond rebellion and the fear at the time of his writing that further interventions still threatened, Sidney's own interpretation of the current crisis was resolutely secular and domestic: the product neither of confessional strife nor of foreign intrigue, the Desmond rebellion was caused by the machinations of internal faction. The one passage in the memoir in which Sidney adverts at all to the existence of religious dissent in Ireland is in itself surprising. While Sidney was in Limerick late in 1575 'there came three or four bishops of the provinces of Cashel and Tuam which bishops (albeit they were Papists) submitted themselves unto the queen's majesty, and unto me her deputy, acknowledging that they held all their temporal patrimony of the queen's majesty, and desired humbly that they might (by her highness) be inducted into their ecclesiastical prelacy. Here was some hold between the bishops and me, too long to be recited; for they stood still upon *Salve suo ordine* &c., and I of the queen's absolute authority' (p. 86). There was disagreement here clearly, but it is equally clear that even as late as 1583 Sidney seemed to regard such disputes not as fundamental but as amenable to resolution through personal contact and negotiation.

In contrast to Sidney's lack of interest in critical ethnographic observation, where claims on his behalf have always been overstated, this apparent coolness in regard to religious reform, despite his active engagements with such matters during his time of service, raises important questions concerning the memoir's relation to the factual record which require address. And similar issues arise in an even more urgent form when the secular policies which he actually initiated and pursued as viceroy are compared with the account presented in the memoir. For, despite the agreement of most recent scholars that Sidney was above all committed to the advancement of English rule in Ireland through legal, institutional and tenurial reform, the memoir appears to be disturbingly silent on such matters.[26] Though Sidney was the first governor actually to succeed in establishing provincial councils in Munster and in Connacht (a disappointed ambition of many of his predecessors), he makes little of this achievement in the memoir. He mentions in passing his intent to establish councils as a means of overcoming factions in the provinces, but offers no account of their character, their powers, nor of the manifold troubles and frustrations which had attended their establishment; and indeed the first individuals to hold the office of provincial president, Sir Edward Fitton and Sir John Perrot, are introduced only as agents in Sidney's narrative of military encounters. Even more curious is the apparent absence of discussion of the major policy initiative that formed the centrepiece of Sidney's last term of office, the elaborate effort at feudal and tenurial reform which he termed 'composition'.[27]

Composition does appear rather obliquely in Sidney's account of his late troubles with the Palesmen, which he depicts as a struggle to defend the prerogative of the Crown. But the underlying radicalism of his plan, which sought to raise a tax without parliamentary consent, against which the Palesmen were reacting, is never fully acknowledged. The radical character of similar schemes in Munster and Connacht is likewise obscured in his general account of the military adventures of his agents in those provinces. Moreover, in contrast to the elaborate explanatory memoranda which he and his adviser Edmund Tremayne drafted during the time when the idea of composition was first being formulated, the Sidney of the memoir is remarkably taciturn regarding the aims and operating assumptions of his bold initiative.[28] It was, he says, 'a great enterprise', and its introduction in 1575 the fulfilment of 'an old conceit of mine own' (p. 94). There is something important, clearly, lurking underneath these coy references. Yet the condensed manner in which he treats the intrigues and compromises that he was obliged to undergo in the early 1570s in order to gain the right to enact his grand design gives rise to one of the most obscure and disingenuous passages in the entire memoir:

> Now (Sir), I know not by what destiny, but ill enough I am sure for me, nor how things went and were governed when I went from thence, but I was not at home many months unsent for, for consultation sake for the affairs of that country, and caused to attend at the court, and in that sort oftentimes to my great charge, without any

> allowance; for there was some in great authority that had no will that I should go thither; and so upon every letter of *omnia bene*, I was dismissed without reward; and being thus wearied with often sending for to no purpose, I resolved to go thither again; the place I protest, before God, which I cursed, hated and detested, and yet confess with supposition that I could do that which had not been done before, and in great hope hit where others had missed. (p. 81)

With its multiple non sequiturs and evasions, telescoping the years between 1572 and 1575 and passing silently over the intensive politicking in which he had engaged during that time, this is a strikingly obscure sequence. But it is also highly revealing. It betrays, of course, Sidney's continuing embarrassment with the great though controversial 'conceit'—the policy of composition—which had brought his Irish career to ruin and left him morally suspect thereafter. Yet what this unusually clumsy piece of passagework highlights is the very great rhetorical success of Sidney's narrative technique elsewhere. While narrative, that is to say, occasionally failed him, in general it provided him with the ideal means of emphasising such matters as now engaged his primary interest—places, individuals and, of course, events—while diminishing the significance of other issues—questions of policy formulation and assessment—which were clearly better addressed within an analytical rather than a discursive mode and could therefore easily be passed over. What his rare lapse has laid bare, then, was the essential success of Sidney's narrative mode as a medium of inclusion and exclusion. For despite its apparently innocent factuality, Sidney's memoir, like all autobiographies, functioned implicitly as a deeply selective rhetorical strategy, alternately revealing and concealing matter from its readers in a manner which, whether he had set about it consciously or not, was inescapably self-serving.

In approaching the memoir from this formalist perspective, however, and to read it simply as some sorry exercise in deception and self-defence would be to miss the point. For the operation of his narrative's filtering process is considerably more subtle in the rest of Sidney's text than in the singular passage just discussed. Close comparison of the memoir's sequence with the independent surviving evidence of Sidney's actual service in Ireland reveals surprisingly few chronological deviations; and the remarkable accord between the memoir and the independent record is often so perfect that one must surmise that, despite Sidney's claim to be writing from memory, he had to hand a letter-book containing copies of correspondence, or at least a register of letters received and dispatched. Yet it is this very compatibility that makes the few divergences that actually occur appear all the more interesting and suggestive of an authorial process more complex and profound than a simple intent to deceive.[29]

The account of Sidney's first tour of duty from January 1566 to July 1567 follows faithfully the record of contemporary correspondence, but with one important exception. In the midst of his account of the pursuit of Shane O'Neill there occurs one revealing transposition placing Shane's rout at the hands of the O'Donnells at Farsetmore before presenting a colourful narration of his winter forays against O'Neill which, Sidney claims, eventually reduced Shane to his fatal decision to seek aid from the Scots. The sequence, in fact, was quite the reverse: Sidney's occasional winter raids had done little to damage Shane, and it was Farsetmore (8 May 1567) that presaged his ruin. On one level this alteration may be read simply as an old soldier's vanity; but, as we shall see, Sidney's desire to emphasise the importance of his personal encounters with the great powers of the island reflects the deepest imperatives of the text as a whole.

In his second tour further divergences appear. His account here traces his efforts to suppress the rebellion of the Geraldines and the Butlers from August 1568 down to April 1570. At that point he announces the summoning of a parliament. But the parliament itself, which had been the keystone of the reform programme with which he had reassumed office, had been sitting since January 1569 and was about to commence its fifth session, by which time the bulk of its most important pieces of legislation had either been passed or dropped.[30]

Even then, the summoning of parliament is mentioned only in passing amidst Sidney's continuing relation of military events down to the beginning of 1571, and it is only at the close of this account that he returns to it. 'Now approached the parliament,' he writes, giving the impression that the subject was indeed being allotted its appropriate chronological place. But the ensuing discussion never moves beyond the mere listing of beneficial acts passed, combined with some comments on the malice of those who sought to frustrate their passage. This is not to claim that Sidney's mis-sequencing here was either deliberately misleading or even intentional. It may have been so; but equally he may simply have found that, given his commitment to narrative, this was the easiest way to organise his account. But the speculation is superfluous, for, either way, this late choice of emphasis is a striking indicator of a change of priorities between the drafter of a major programme of legislative reform who governed Ireland in 1568–71, and the subsequent narrator of the memoir.

A third chronological deviation, though even less obvious, is equally revealing. In his account of his last term in office Sidney again follows the independent record with an apparently rigorous consistency, tracing his perambulations of the island from September 1575 to February 1577. Up to that point the narrative records the occurrences of a highly successful tour, one that was apparently all too successful: 'for that the country being reduced into such quiet as they mistrusted no wars to come' the nobles and gentry of the Pale mounted a campaign of complaint against the extortion of Sidney and his garrison in order that they might be relieved of any obligation to feed and supply them (p. 92). Such an explanation of the origins of the movement against Sidney's attempt to impose composition in the Pale is convenient. But it ignores the fact that discontent had arisen immediately upon Sidney's arrival in Ireland with his very first attempt to substitute for the onerous and amorphous set of exactions known collectively as 'the cess' his own tax of composition. Opposition mounted throughout 1576 and early 1577 and was based not upon some novel confidence that the English garrison was no longer necessary, but upon the genuine fear that Sidney was proposing a non-parliamentary land tax which would bind the freeholders of the Pale in perpetuity.[31]

Sidney's discomfiture with an episode which had led even his close friends to doubt his wisdom and intentions at that time may underlie this further departure from the chronological record. Yet, as before, the implication that Sidney was deliberately attempting to skew the evidence remains both untestable and beside the point. Had he wished, Sidney was certainly capable of defending his conduct in regard to composition, for he had done so ably enough in the past.[32] But in the manner of those earlier ripostes, such a case would clearly have been most effectively advanced in a forensic fashion, setting forth the nature of the problems for which his policy was devised, defending the appropriateness of its techniques, and itemising the political and financial benefits which it had earned. As a mode of defence, sequential narrative was, then, of distinctly limited value: it might on occasion obscure the truth from the uninitiated; but presented to more engaged or more hostile readers, it was a highly vulnerable strategy, and in retaining it Sidney committed himself to risks which at once diminished his chances of mounting a strong response to his adversaries while exposing him to charges of deliberate obfuscation. That, despite its obvious strategic weaknesses, Sidney persisted with it is evidence that, within his own mind, narrative still remained the most appropriate vehicle for the representation of his experience of Ireland, and evidence therefore that, in this his last major statement on Ireland, he was intent on something more ambitious than a mere defence of his record.

From this more positive view of narrative's capabilities, one central purpose for which the form was especially suited becomes immediately obvious. This was Sidney's determination to expose the persistently evil influence exercised over Irish affairs by the powerful and ostensibly unimpeachable figure, Thomas Butler, tenth Earl of Ormond. Sidney announces the role which Ormond is being allotted in his story almost at the very outset. Within a year of his appointment Sidney is about to deliver the *coup de grace to* the rebel Shane O'Neill: 'But Sir — *Diabolus nunquam dormit*, for now the Earl of Ormond applied the Queen with such complaints against me . . . as I was forced to leave my northern actions . . . which prolonged the life and wars of O'Neill, greatly to the queen's charge' (p. 49). First announced here, Ormond's guilt, both for the continuing disorders of Ireland and for the waste of royal revenues, is laced throughout the entire text. It was Ormond who both directly and indirectly undermined all of Sidney's plans for the reform of Ireland, and whose brothers' rebellion—recounted in great detail in the narrative—wrecked Sidney's plans for the government of Ireland after the defeat of Shane O'Neill; Ormond who incited the malice of others and intimidated the faint-hearted into silence; Ormond who professed hypocritically to love peace and order but in whose territories lay the very 'sink of criminality and baseness'. And, astonishingly, it was Ormond, rather than Desmond, who was really responsible for the rebellion now raging (pp. 49, 52, 57–8).

The malevolence of the diabolical earl forms such a leitmotif in the narrative that it seems easy to conclude that it was his denunciation, above any other consideration, which prompted Sidney to write. Sidney's grounds for hating Ormond were ample. For the earl had indeed greatly frustrated his first term in office, especially in regard to his plans for a provincial council in Munster; his brothers' rebellion had indeed consumed Sidney's second service in Ireland; and Sidney was right to suspect that Ormond was an encourager of several of the complaints raised against Sidney's composition programme in the late 1570s. Now at the time of writing Ormond had just been appointed governor of Munster, enjoying complete military and political authority in the region.[33] Sidney's strident anti-Ormondist polemic can thus be seen as an important contribution to a gathering campaign against the earl which was being mounted both by English officials in Dublin and in Whitehall, who feared that, in the wake of a successful outcome in Munster, Ormond would enjoy unprecedented influence in the post-rebellion province and might even be granted the Irish viceroyalty from a grateful monarch, the first Irish-born figure to enjoy the office since the Kildare rebellion of 1534.[34]

Sidney's desire to damage his old adversary cannot be doubted, and the prospects of Ormond's elevation in the aftermath of his own failure to gain reappointment to office must certainly have spurred his indignation. Yet as an anti-Ormondist blast, it has to be admitted, Sidney's text was hardly perfect. Its invective is, in the first place, painfully obvious. Sidney's portrayal of himself as a good servitor brought down by the evil earl may have brought him some personal comfort. But for independent readers, uncommitted to his cause, it would certainly have done much to undercut the status of his allegations as objective criticisms: for Elizabethans were as capable as any generation of discerning the whiff of sour grapes.[35] In this regard too, Sidney's undisguised defence of and sympathy for the irreconcilable rebel Sir John of Desmond could hardly have strengthened the anti-Ormondist cause. But in any case there were for the purposes of polemic many alternative weapons other than autobiography—an expert's report, detailing the subject's conduct during his years of office, an ostensibly impersonal examination of the allegations made against him, or even a list of the disreputable figures he had pardoned or protected (all of which had been used in by Sidney and others in similar campaigns the past)—which would clearly have served a better turn here. But once again Sidney doggedly settled for narrative.

Moreover, while Ormond is presented as the principal villain of the viceroy's tale, he is, it should be emphasised, by no means the only one. For other figures people Sidney's text who, though they re-enact in their lesser fashion the malicious, self-interested and destructive role of which Ormond is the archetype, represent other malignant influences and who combined lessen the rhetorical thrust of a simple attack on Ormond. There is, for instance, Shane O'Neill, the unbridled tyrant with whom the text begins, and later the devious and treacherous Earl of Clanrickard who did so much to undermine Sidney in the west. But evil radiates not only from the Irish: the rash ambitions of the Earl of Essex and his violent way of proceeding parallels the impetuosity and arrogance of several of the Irish lords, and, most strikingly, it is the English-born Lord Chancellor, Sir William Gerrard, who comes closest to Ormond in Sidney's list of obstructers of the good government of Ireland (pp. 79, 93, 96). Individually, none of these can equal Ormond in iniquity; yet by their inclusion in a gallery of bad subjects, Sidney makes it clear that he had more than one grudge to settle, or one target in mind.

Thus, however timely its appearance, it would be unwise to identify the memoir as nothing more than a clumsy contribution to an English campaign against an ascendant Irish earl. Though it might have been deemed useful as such by some who may have encouraged Sidney to commit himself to paper, there is no need to assume that Sir Henry would have meekly accepted such a commission had it indeed been proposed. Rather, it is seems better to accept that, whatever uses others might have wished to make of it, Sidney's account, peopled with knaves, fools and friends among whom the former sadly predominated, constituted nothing more nor less than an accurate reflection of the landscape of his Irish memory as he reviewed it in 1583. Read in this manner, Sidney's reiterated story of the hero's encounter with persons good and evil may seem both self-serving and *simpliste*; but it is deceptively so. For closer attention to the patterns of his narrative reveals a series of interrelated dramatic tropes underlying and recurring throughout his text which not only serve as organising principles sustaining its implicit coherence, but also reveal his deepest assumptions concerning the nature of the problems facing English government in Ireland and the most effective means of addressing them.

Of these organising tropes, the most obvious is travel. From beginning to end the imperative force behind the chronological development of the narrative is supplied by the viceroy's apparently ceaseless circuiting of the island. Ireland, that is to say, is represented not as a set of contingent cultural and ethnic zones, as so many later observers and historians have characterised it, but as an almost continuous road, traversing and connecting the island's different lordships, along which the viceroy routinely travelled in the discharge of his duties. It may be observed that such a plot was simply a genuine representation of the state of affairs, reflecting more closely than the models of modern scholars what the Irish viceroys actually did. In itself that is a point worth establishing. But the matter is more complex still. For the perambulative trope in the narrative not only determined the sequence in which all of the historical events of the viceroyalty were to be recorded; it also, in a barely perceptible way, assigned the relative status that was to be accorded to each. And here a subtle innovation can be noted. The presentation of a hierarchical roster, listing the most powerful lordships secured or defeated and the most dangerous left outstanding, was a more obvious manner of demonstrating the viceroy's achievements, and was the manner in which such reports had frequently been composed in the past. But the adoption here of the alternative sequence of the road overturned such orderings, permitting each of the viceroy's encounters to be reorganised into a simple catalogue of events that may be summarised as battles won, treaties negotiated, friendships formed and setbacks suffered.

This subtle categorical revision was reinforced by descriptive omission. For just as Sidney's account offers little cultural or ethnographic comment on the regions through which he passed—making little comment on the supposedly primitive economic conditions of rural Ireland in the manner that historians have been led to expect—so he provides little detail on the practical logistics of his travels. Thus the procurement of guides, the cutting of passes, the collection of forage, etc., the standard matters discussed in such recorded itineraries, receive little attention. Instead the line of the road-narrative is pared down to one single, reiterated event, the encounter: the battle on some occasions, the friendly entertainment on others, but, most commonly of all, the negotiation. In each of Sidney's journeys, that is to say, the same simple diorama is depicted over and over: the viceroy is met by the lord of the territories through which he passes, the lord (more or less willingly) submits, negotiations take place in which the lord promises fealty, offers a revenue and is reconciled to the viceroy, who, with some retrospective praise of the good service and loyalty of the figure concerned, goes on to record the next encounter.

It is in relation to these recurring tropes of his narrative—a sequence of similar and generally positive encounters between the governor and innumerable individual lords as he made his perambulation throughout the country—that the significance of the apparently dominant theme of the text—Sidney's preoccupation with the evil machinations of the Earl of Ormond—must now be revisited. For traversing and disrupting these multiple reconciliations between viceroy and local lords, which the narrative represents as normal, is the malign influence of faction which, through intrigue and intimidation in the localities and the exercise of overweening influence at court, has exercised a wholly abnormal effect on the governing process. Commentary on the corrosive effects of faction on the body politic as a whole was a familiar feature of the political thought of Sidney's time, and there is nothing to suggest that his narrative has any new perspective to offer on the problem in general. But in placing the phenomenon so close to the centre of his autobiographical account, Sidney exhibits the degree to which he perceived it to be fundamental to the problem of Irish politics. In this apprehension he himself was not particularly original. Indeed, as in so much else, he seems to have followed here the more consciously articulated analysis of his predecessor in the Irish office, Thomas Radcliffe, third Earl of Sussex.

During his miserable term as viceroy Sussex had worked toward an important reversal in the conventional understanding of the Irish problem. That view had long asserted that the root cause of the country's lawlessness and poverty lay in the pervasive exploitation by the island's great powers of arbitrary military exactions and taxes (known summarily as 'coyne and livery') and of the size and burden of the great private armies which underpinned the system. Remove coyne and livery, the orthodox view held, and the sources of Ireland's incivility would be quenched. In practice, opinions differed as to how this might be done, with some voices advocating direct confrontation and others stressing the efficacy of persuasion. It was the latter view, most strongly represented by the English governor Sir Anthony St Leger, which had prevailed in the 1540s and early 1550s, and it was this brand of orthodoxy that by 1560 Sussex had felt obliged to challenge. Bypassing the conventional wisdom on coyne and livery, Sussex argued that Ireland's fundamental political problem was not the system itself, but the great dynastic factions which it sustained and which opposed every effort to dissolve it. No reform strategy, of whatever hue, would prevail until these factions had first been dismantled.[36]

Sussex had identified the Geraldines, the followers of the house of Kildare, as the focus of evil in the Irish world, and had consequently regarded their opponents, the Butlers of Ormond and their clients, as susceptible to reform by persuasion. Succeeding him as a rival, Sidney, not unnaturally, had reversed the relationship regarding the Geraldines (even the house of Desmond) with relative tolerance while reserving all his vitriol for the hated Ormond. But implicitly he had accepted Sussex's revisionist analysis in its essentials, acknowledging that the problem of Ireland was not broadly cultural—resting upon the evil system of coyne and livery with all its unhappy social and economic consequences—and accepting instead that it was narrowly political, residing in the capacity of powerful interests to obstruct their inferiors' natural desire to attain peace and prosperity by submitting themselves to the laws and customs of the English Crown.

It was this adoption of Sussex's specifically political analysis that makes sense of what otherwise might be seen as the untidy and unsatisfactory character of Sidney's anti-Ormondist polemic. For while Ormond was far and away the figure most destructive of the common good, he was not, we have seen Sidney allow, the only one. Rather, what the subversive Palesmen, the ambitious Chancellor Gerrard and the reckless Earl of Essex share in common with the wicked Ormond was both a desire to place their own special interests above that of the commonweal, and an ability on crucial occasions to exert such a force over other individuals and groups in order to manipulate events in favour of their own selfish or destructive aspirations.

This assumption of the primacy of the political in Sidney's understanding of Ireland suggests a view of the manner in which the country might be made amenable to English government that is both simple in appearance and yet loaded with complex implicit assumptions of which Sidney himself may only have been half-aware. Without the contagion of faction, Sidney seems to argue, the (re-)establishment of good relations between the Crown and its Irish subjects could be achieved by patient negotiations with the viceroy which would establish a mutually agreed power relationship between both parties. Sidney's optimism here was not unqualified, and there is no sense in the memoir that he regarded the success of negotiations as guaranteed. Yet as a whole the narrative seems to sustain his confidence that, without the interruption of destructive forces fuelled by faction and political ambition, this would be the normal outcome. Some contrasting examples will illustrate the point. From the beginning Sir Hugh O'Donnell established a firm and lasting relationship with the governor because of his own realistic estimation of his disputed position among the other powers of Tír Conaill. By contrast, the irksome 'ox' of Thomond had illusory pretensions to power until Sidney controlled him by bolstering the standing of other more dependable O'Briens in the lordship. Turlough Luineach O'Neill was a chronically unstable but not wholly unregenerate figure who was at length brought to negotiate by pressure, inducement and especially through the shrewdness of the remarkable Agnes Campbell. Such instances defined the spectrum of the successful negotiating process. Complete breakdowns occurred only when extraneous factors interposed: Shane O'Neill's tyranny, Sir William Gerrard's vanity, Essex's violence, and Ormond's insatiable malice.

The presupposition of the normality of negotiation and the abnormality of total conflict did not necessarily imply a naïve view of the Irish political character on Sidney's part. His mind, as we have seen, was resistant to all categorical analyses of human disposition, and the tone of the memoir as a whole seems to convey the attitude of one who takes men as he finds them. Yet beneath such an ostensibly *simpliste* view of the negotiating process, and underpinning Sidney's accounts of its more and less successful instances, a coherent (though perhaps unconscious) conceptual framework of considerable complexity can be discerned through a set of three related interpretative elements which recur throughout his narrative.

The first of these is Sidney's preoccupation with the disaggregation of power among the Gaelic lordships. Expressed here in the author's indefatigable interest in nominating the most minor territorial units, Sidney's general concern with deconstructing the largest lordships of Gaelic Ireland into the smallest integers of territorial power has sometimes been seen merely as an instance of his determination to divide and rule.[37] Yet Sidney's attitude was, in reality, rather more sophisticated. It should be noted that he was on occasions willing to tolerate quite large blocs as fundamental units of power, as, for example, in the lordships of O'Donnell, MacCarthy More and even, though more circumspectly, Turlough Luineach O'Neill. Thus his drive towards fragmentation was far from absolute. For Sidney's deep distrust of the larger lordships lay not primarily in his fear of the potential threat they posed to his government, but rather in his sense of their own inherent instability, of the overreaching nature of their claims over lesser lords that regularly provoked resistance, repression and all the disorders to which, he believed, Gaelic Ireland was chronically prone. It is clear, moreover, that for Sidney the pernicious nature of such claims was not merely an abstraction, an offence against the ideals of natural justice. It was a practically demonstrable fact that could be measured in each case in the lords' ability effectively to levy and collect such rents as they deemed their due. The more unrealistic the claims, the greater the trouble they provoked; and, conversely, the more stability enjoyed by a lord, the clearer was the evidence that his claims were well founded. Thus Sidney's determination to dismantle the great agglomerations of Gaelic Ireland and to reduce their claims to levels correlative with their ability peacefully to extract them was not, for him, part of some deep plan to overturn the political *status quo*, but merely an attempt to discover and confirm it.

It is this identification of the relationship between accurate fiscal assessment and political stability which also sustained the second of Sidney's recurring interpretative assumptions: his belief that at the core of each of his negotiations, and guaranteeing their permanence, there should be an agreement on the part of the lords to yield a certain rent to the Crown. Again, such a preoccupation with revenue can easily be interpreted as just another imperialist ploy to mulct the natives. But here also Sidney's attitude is somewhat less simple. His desire to raise funds and, more significantly, his pride in claiming that at the time of his writing such revenues were still being received are obvious throughout the text. Yet, despite some self-congratulation, Sidney's interest lay not with the actual amount of revenues raised—which he refers to only in an imprecise and unsystematic manner—but with the fact that they were raised at all. Had Sidney been primarily concerned with registering profit for the Crown, he might, as he himself and several of his predecessors had previously done, have made his case more effectively by drawing up a detailed quantitative schedule of the sums involved.[38] That he chose not to do so is evidence that on this occasion Sidney was concerned not simply with the practical value of revenues, but with their larger political and constitutional significance. For buried within Sidney's identification of an equation between fealty and an ability to pay rent there lay an unstated constitutional theory, most of whose elements were, for his time, entirely conventional but which at its edge seemed to imply a quite significant development.

One of the precepts underlying Sidney's unspoken constitutional thought was simply the belief that an ability to hold and manage land offered primary grounds for a claim to political status. Another presumed that a willingness to yield a portion of such wealth in return for recognition and protection from any other exaction constituted the basis of a compact between the sovereign (as represented by the viceroy) and a potential subject. All of this was founded on the bedrock of English constitutional thought. But then Sidney espoused a further precept—a condition that appeared to imply that the validity of this compact between subject and sovereign should be regularly confirmed by a tax, the peaceful collection of which would serve as proof that the original agreement had not been disrupted by any individual ambition or external influence. It was in this final elaboration—the condition that fealty required regular fiscal confirmation—that the most original aspect of Sidney's embryonic constitutional thought was to be found. For this, little support could be found in conventional views of the English constitution. Instead, we can now see, it had specific origins in Sidney's conviction that such a test was particularly pressing in Ireland, where the singularly potent force of faction had shadowed the norm of political stability with the constant threat of disruption. And it was on the basis of this novel insight that the third and most individual assumption of Sidney's Irish narrative rested.

Because the natural development of reconciliation between the Crown and its potential subjects had been disrupted in Ireland through the opposing force of a pervasive and deeply rooted factionalism, Sidney believed it necessary that a new countervailing force be introduced to withstand faction's power. This was to be supplied, in the first instance, by the arms of an English garrison. Once more this central feature of Sidney's narrative can easily be put down to crude imperialist ambition: military rule. But here too the matter is more complex. The crucial role played by indigenous forces such as O'Donnell, Fitz-Patrick of Upper Ossory, the Inchiquin O'Briens and even (the lost and limiting case) Sir John of Desmond in providing such countervailing force is acknowledged throughout Sidney's text, underlining his recognition that the required force need not necessarily be supplied by the Crown. It is, however, the agents of a new royal garrison that feature most prominently in his account. Yet even here the most obvious characteristic of such a dedicated military establishment—its strength in horse and foot, its fire-power and ordnance, its strategic deployment, questions of tactics and training, and matters of logistics, pay and supply—are hardly considered at all. Instead the army is presented by Sidney not as a single entity or institution, but, as in the case of the Gaelic lords, discretely. It appears, that is, as a set of individuals—William Piers, William Collier, Nicholas Malby, Thomas Masterson, etc.—whose distinguished service was recorded by Sidney not in terms of territories conquered or colonies founded, but in their role in enforcing his treaties with several native lords in various regions and in ensuring that thereafter the spirit of those treaties would be honoured. Both in terms of the narrative and of the reality it claimed to represent, these new men of force were designed to serve neither as a juggernaut of conquest nor as a standing army, but as a set of precision tools supplementing and confirming the disaggregating negotiations which constituted the central theme of Sidney's narration.

It is these same 'good soldiers', however, who feature prominently in what to modern eyes is one of the ugliest passages in the entire memoir, the account of the hunting down of the midlands rebel Rory Oge O'More. This section of the memoir, read in conjunction with the representation of Sidney in John Derricke's *Image of Irelande* (1581) and with some circumstantial evidence linking him to the massacre of Mullaghmast in 1578, has recently been presented as proof of Sidney's espousal of radically violent and even genocidal policies toward the native Irish.[39] The validity of such a claim can be properly assessed only in relation to all of the evidence upon which it is based; but it is clear that, within the context of the memoir itself, the account of Rory Oge was intended to convey a quite specific message. The descendant of the dispossessed lords of Laois, who had formerly been favoured by Sidney, Rory had, through the noxious influence of the Earl of Ormond, broken out again in rebellion, consolidating his power through intimidation and terror. A typical representative of the unstable political environment in which Sidney had been obliged to operate, Rory was, however, susceptible to the same medication which had worked so well in other areas: violent pursuit by the old soldiers who knew best how to deal with him and his kind. Yet, significantly, principal credit for Rory's destruction is given by Sidney not to the English servitors, but to the Gaelic Irish lord of Upper Ossory, Sir Barnaby FitzPatrick, whose long suffering at the hands of Ormond and his creatures had rendered him particularly suitable for such a service. Typically, however, neither FitzPatrick nor Sidney had received the recognition they deserved, and, as was the case with the arch-traitor O'Neill with which Sidney opened his narrative, an uncomprehending court contemptuously dismissed Sidney's efforts. Thus in the nature of the threat he posed, in the manner in which that threat was met, and finally in the ignorance and malice with which the entire affair was treated at Whitehall, the hunting of Rory Oge encapsulated everything which Sidney was attempting to express about his sorry Irish experience: it served as an epitome of his entire text.

In emphasising his disregard for conventional ethnic or cultural explanations of the Irish condition, and his absorption of concepts of power and force as effective diagnostic tools, such an analysis of the ageing Sidney's distinctive and complex literary testament may impress later readers with a sense of the remarkable modernity of his mind. It is tempting to speculate as to the origins of this intellectual development: Sidney's apparent freedom from tradition as well as his endorsement of the conceptual perspectives and language of abstract power will doubtless suggest to some a familiarity with a cast of thought that his contemporaries would have described delicately as Italianate. As is the case with so many literate Elizabethans, no firm evidence can be found to prove that Sidney had actually read Machiavelli. Given his almost certain knowledge of Guicciardini's *Storia d'Italia* and the early acquaintance of his son Philip with a range of Machiavelli's works, it seems probable that he did.[40] The memoranda drawn up for him by his adviser Edmund Tremayne in the early 1570s suggest both in their grasp of the political role of the army and the efficacy of coercion as a medium of political reform a more than passing conversance with Machiavellian thought.[41] But, since no direct references can be found in the memoir itself, suggestions of this kind must, in the absence of stronger evidence, remain inconclusive.

Equally inconclusive, though hardly less tantalising, are the implications arising out of Sidney's perception of an ideal political regime in Ireland. Had it actually been established, Sidney's new Irish polity in which political legitimacy was secured on the basis of an ability to collect and yield a regular revenue to the Crown and in which the tax regime was sustained by a permanent military force in the provinces would certainly have represented a radical departure from contemporary English constitutional thought. It is possible, indeed, to see within it anticipations of the reconstruction of political and fiscal relations in France in the late sixteenth and early seventeenth centuries which has become known to historians as 'absolutism'. It may be noted in this regard that Sidney's desire to co-opt a compliant or supportive regional aristocracy as one of the foundations of the regime does indeed seem to anticipate what the most sophisticated modern analyses have identified as an essential constituent of the fully developed French model.[42] The retrospective attribution of anticipation is, however, an incongruous and inherently dubious historical exercise, best not pursued too dogmatically.

But, whatever their attractions, speculations concerning the origins and implications of Sidney's thought are not only necessarily inconclusive, they are also in the present context largely irrelevant. For just as he did not seek to write a comprehensive autobiography, nor merely an anti-Ormondist polemic, nor a schedule of revenues and lands gained, neither was Sidney attempting to compose a coherent political treatise disguised in another form. Rather, we must finally grant that the form which he actually adopted and persisted with over several drafts in spite of all its inherent difficulties was the one best suited to him, not for the purposes which subsequent commentators have prescribed for him, but as the most appropriate vehicle of expression as Sidney himself sought to comprehend the central import of his peculiar Irish experience. By the distinctive cultural, political and constitutional problems it presented to him in his attempt to re-establish English government there, Ireland had enabled Sidney's quick intelligence to cut loose from its conventional moorings by suggesting the possibility of a boldly original approach toward the problems of viceregal rule as whole. And the real, if patchy, success of this approach had revealed to him also a glimpse of a radically different understanding of the means by which in general the stability of the state might be sustained within the flux of the political process. But as the locus also of the frustrations, defeats and misunderstandings that had blighted his career, Ireland had equally exposed the flawed and inchoate character of this hard-earned revelation. The outcome, then, for Sidney had been paradox: a repeated experience of insight crossed by confusion, of initiative stymied by paralysis, of achievement buried by disregard. And it was as a means of disentangling these knots of contradiction that, for all his audacity, had been the hallmarks of his viceroyalties, and of making some sense of the tumult of his years in Ireland, that Sidney reverted to that primary cognitive exercise from whence all attempts at imposing order on experience must start. He undertook the composition of a detailed, carefully sequential, personal narrative.

Editorial Note

Three manuscript copies of the memoir are extant. Two are in the Carew Manuscripts at Lambeth Palace Library in vol. 601, f. 89ff and a second shorter version in vol. 628, f. 318ff. A third, the text edited here, is a separate volume in the State Papers, Domestic series in the Public Record Office, London (reference SP 12, vol. 159). The autograph draft referred to by Sidney in the present text has not survived, and—significantly perhaps—the extensive Sidney private archive housed in the Centre for Kentish Studies, Maidstone, contains no copy. Carew 628 is clearly the earliest surviving version and is without the introductory letter that precedes the present text. Carew 601 includes some minor material excised from SP 12. I have added these silently in the present edition (e.g. 'brake his battle' for 'brake him', p. 48), and occasionally I have preferred its scribal readings (e.g. 'worthy honest' for 'worshipful honest', p. 52). It is, however, without several of the corrections, marginal notes (some in Sidney's hand) and additional matter contained in the SP 12 version. Thus while little of substance distinguishes them, and while Carew 601 may be a later copy from an earlier draft, it is clear that the SP 12 manuscript was Sidney's latest working draft.

This SP 12 manuscript has previously been edited and published with some brief introductory comments and extensive antiquarian notes by Herbert F. Hore over several volumes of the *Ulster Journal of Archaeology*, 1st series, iii (1855), pp. 33–52, 85–109, 336–57; v (1857), pp. 299–322; viii (1866), pp. 179–95. Hore's transcription was very accurate, and while misreadings, dropped words and occasionally dropped lines occur, I have amended these silently and will draw attention to only the most significant ones here: thus I have inserted 'denied not' for 'denied out' (p. 46), 'captains' for 'counsellors'(p. 50); 'cancerdest' for 'cowerdest' (p. 93) and 'Spain' for 'Scotland' (p. 106). The ideological significance of Hore's omission of the phrase 'most like a slave' (p. 97) has been the subject of some speculation (by Vincent Carey in *Irish Historical Studies*, xxxi (1998–99), p. 318), but the multiplying psychological implications of his mistranscription of 'whores' as 'boars' (p. 94) are best passed over in silence.

On the series editor's advice I have modernised spelling and punctuation and introduced paragraphs as the sense dictated. I have generally regularised capitalisation in accordance with modern usage except where there seemed good reason for preserving Sidney's inconsistencies. I have preserved original spellings of names of persons and places where the orthography may be of phonetic interest and where Sidney's peculiar spelling has been consistent (e.g. Turlo Lenogh). Generally Latin tags and archaic or obscure words have been translated or explained in square brackets.

Sir Henry Sidney's Book
1582 [1583 n.s.]

[PRO, State Papers, Domestic, SP 12, vol. 159]

Dear Sir,

I have understood of late that coldness is thought in me in proceeding in the matter of marriage of our children. In truth (Sir) it is not so, nor so shall it ever be found; for, compremitting [summarising] the consideration of the articles to the earls named by you, and to the Earl of Huntington, I most willingly agree, and protest I joy in the alliance with all my heart.[1] But since, by your letters of the third of January, to my great discomfort I find there is no hope of relief of her Majesty for my decayed estate in her Highness service (for since you give it over, I will never make more means, but say *spes et fortuna valete*).[2] I am the more careful to keep myself able, by sale of part of that which is left, to ransom me out of the servitude I live in for my debts. For as I know, Sir, that it is the virtue which is, or that you suppose is, in my son, that you made choice of him for your daughter, refusing haply far greater and far richer matches than he so was my confidence great, that by your good mean, I might have obtained some small reasonable suit of her Majesty; and therefore I nothing regarded any present gain; for if I had, I might have received a great sum of money for my good will of my son's marriage, greatly to the relief of my private biting necessity.

For truly (Sir) I respect nothing by provision or prevention of that which may come hereafter as this. I am not so unlusty but that I may be so employed, as I may have occasion to sell land to redeem myself out of prison, nor yet am I so old, nor my wife so healthy, but that she may die, and I marry again and get children, or think I get some. If such a thing should happen, God's law and man's law will that both one and other may be provided for. Many other accidents of regard might be alleged, but neither the forewritten, nor any that may be thought of to come, do I respect, but only to stay land to sell, to acquit me of the thraldom I now live in for my debts.[3]

But, good Sir, since her Majesty will not be moved to reward me, nor removed from her opinion but that the two great and high offices which I have so long and so often wielded may and ought to be a sufficient satisfaction for any my service done in them or elsewhere, give me leave, patiently on your part, though over tediously on mine, somewhat to write to you of those offices, and of my service in them; and though I play a little too boldly in person of mine own herald, yet pardon me, it is my first fault of this kind.

Three times her Majesty hath sent me her Deputy into Ireland, and in every of the three times I sustained a great and a violent rebellion, every one of which I subdued, and (with honourable peace) left the country in quiet. I returned from each of those three Deputations three thousand pounds worse than I went.

The first deputation* was against Shane O'Neill,[4] the Arch-traitor, who not only had usurped and peaceably did keep under him the whole estate of Tyrone, being O'Neill's country, but also had subdued and pulled to him all such potentates and landlords in Ulster as he termed his urriaghes [*uir-ríthe*: literally sub-kings, vassal lords], viz, the captain of Farney, MacMahon, Magennis, MacCartan, O'Hanlon, and Maguire; all which his father had renounced to make any claim to.[5] He had forcibly patronised himself in all Lecale, and all the lordships of Sir Nicholas Bagenal,[6] and the Ards, which are great countries. He held in his subjection the lordship and lords of Clandeboy and the Route. The Scots of the Glens he held in pay, and they were his mercenary soldiers. The Queen had nothing in possession in all this large tract of land but the miserable town of Carrickfergus, whose goods he would take as oft as he listed, and force the poor people to redeem their own cows with their own wine. He held the county of Louth in such awe as he made the most of them to pay him tribute, called there black rent, or else by stealth or force he would plague them. Finally he exiled [Calvagh] O'Donnell,[7] Lord of Tirconell, and drove him into England, where he craved and obtained letters for aid. This O'Donnell was and is lord of as great a country as his, on which he totally tyrannised, possessing all his castles, which were many and strong, and put under his subjection all the potentates of the same dominion, namely O'Doherty, O'Boyle, O'Gallaghar, the three grand captains of galloglas called MacSweenys of

---

* Marginal note: 'In my first passage, I lost by shipwreck the most of my houshold stuff and utensils, my wife's whole apparel and all her jewels, many horses and stable stuff, etc.'

Fanad, Banagh and Ne Do [*Doe*], all which he either held in prison, or let out, detaining their best hostages.

With this monstrous monarchal Tyrant of all Ulster I made war. And in truth he was mighty, for he had of Scots and Irish seven thousand men that wore weapon. I had but seventeen hundred, with three hundred Berwick soldiers. I advanced into the rebel's country the 22nd of September 1566; I wasted and destroyed all or the most part of Tyrone; the old Maguire [Seán] died in my camp, but I possessed his brother [Cúchonnacht] in his country, taking oath and hostage of him for his loyalty and fealty. I passed without boat or bridge the dangerous rivers of Omagh,* Darg and Finn; at last I came to the great water, or sea arm, of Lough Foyle, where I found boats, as I had appointed, to convey me and my army over; and so I left Tyrone and entered Tirconnell, where I found that renowned and worthy Colonel Mr E[dward] Randolph, with a regiment of seven hundred soldiers full well captained, chosen and appointed.[8]

There of an old church I made a new fort; and being furnished with men, munition and victual, I left the colonel with his regiment in it, and marched through Tirconnell, a country of seventy miles in length, and somewhere forty broad, full of hard passages and dangerous rivers. By the way I left not one castle in the possession of the rebel, nor unrestored to the right owner. So marching on still, and passing the great water of Assurroo [*Asherow*], and having the castle there called Ballyshannon delivered me, I came to the strong castle of Donegal [*marginal correction*: Donegal before Ballyshannon], standing almost at the west end of Tirconnell, which was yielded to me, where I repossessed the old exiled Calvagh O'Donnell, lord of it and the country, and there, in presence of all the people of his country, received homage and fealty of him, and all potentates of that country before recited, acknowledging that he held his countries and all his seigniories immediately of the Queen's majesty, and her crown imperial, by the rent of £200 sterling

---

* Marginal note: 'Here the rebel with all his power showed himself unto me but fight with me he dared not, and made some *bravata* to my camp; but enter it he could not.'

yearly, and the service of horsemen and footmen (in truth the number is now out of my memory, but great it was) and as often as it should be called for, to serve in Ulster, and to be ready elsewhere at every general hosting in Ireland. This agreement was published, written, indented, signed, sealed and delivered, and by the forenamed great ones witnessed, and when I came home, I registered and enrolled the same, and so it remains of record.

And thus much of Tirconnell, saving in the second time of my deputation, I sent to the now O'Donnell called Hugh, whom after the death of his brother Calvagh I made O'Donnell, for the rent above specified, as well as the arrears, which he denied not, affirming that to pay the yearly rent yearly was to him nor his country any burden, much blaming those which succeeded me for that it was suffered so long to rest in arrears, alleging that his followers were froward, and would be found stubborn to pay such a mass at once as the arrears came to, and therefore desired me to send my sergeant with some force, which I did, whom O'Donnell accompanied as diligently and effectually in gathering of the Queen's rent, as if it had been for himself, made my officers and men good cheer, rewarded them for their pains, and sent me £1,200 in payment of the arrears, which was accounted for and delivered to the Treasurer to her Majesty's use, such was my credit and his love and obedience then.

Then passing by the castle of Bundroyes [*Bundrowes*], then rendered to me, as the castle of Beleek was, I delivered them to O'Donnell, and marched into Carbery, O'Connor Sligo's country, the first part to the north-east of the province of Connacht. There met me O'Rourke, a potentate of Connacht, with certain petty lords of his country, whose names I have forgotten, saving two MacGranylles [*Reynolds*]; they submitted, I accepted and ordered as I did in Tirconell, and so went to Sligo [castle], where the lord of the soil, called O'Connor, made me and mine host great cheer and entertainment, and presented his lordings to me, namely O'Dowd, two MacDonoghs, two O'Haras (distinct additions they have, but I have forgotten them); and O'Hara he brought me to Athlone, and promised to come to me to Dublin. He fell in such love and liking of Englishmen and English government as he vowed to go into England to behold the majesty of our sovereign, which he performed.[9]

From thence I marched on the craggy mountain of the Curlew, a passage bad enough, where I chased and chastised the ancient outlaws of that quarter called Garron Bane;[10] and so descended into the plains of Connacht, and took there the great abbey of Aboyle [*Boyle*], and put a tenant into it, who paid the Queen a good rent for it, and so did as long as I was there; and encamped in MacDermod's country [in County Roscommon], who submitted and was ordered as others before.

From thence to Roscommon, the strong castle of which was with somewhat ado delivered to me, being in the possession of disloyal Irishmen one hundred and sixty years; for so long was it before that it was betrayed, and the English constable and ward murdered, as I found in the Irish chronicles.[11] There I planted a small garrison, which has continued ever since; and what good service the same has done since for the reformation of the province, with continuance of residence, with rent and profit, and how good a town is now built about it, I am sure you know better (by Sir Nicholas Malby's[12] relation) than I can inform you.

Thither came to me O'Connor Dun, O'Connor Ro, O'Bryn, O'Flynn, and O'Flannigan, all with their homage, and of all which I took oath and hostage for their loyalty, and tied them to payment of rent and doing of service, which while I was there was performed and observed.[13]

From thence I went to A[th]lone, where all the lineages of the O'Kellys came to me, and desired to take and hold their lands of the Queen by rent and service, and it was done, and continues to this day.*
Thither came to me the two principal captains of the Annaly, called O'Farroll Boy and O'Farroll Bane—the country is of Connacht—and desired that it might be shired and rented, which was done, by the name of the county of Longford, and were set at four hundred marks a year, which is paid at this day, and service of horse and foot; I gave order

---

* Marginal note: Here came to me the two O'Maddens of both side the Shannon, and submitted themselves and their country, with the strong castle of Meleek.

then for the making of the bridge of A[th]lone, which I finished, a piece found serviceable; I am sure durable it is, and I think memorable.[14]

And thus though I ended my long and painful journey somewhat far in the winter, yet was I not idle the same, nor others though without me (yet directed by me) unoccupied. For the Traitor knowing that I was passed by the great water of Lough Foyle, and the shipping returned, so as I could not but make it a very long journey, before I could come back into the English Pale, he with great force of horsemen invaded the same, and made roads to the very walls of Dreydath [*Drogheda*], where my most dear wife then lay.[15] But he was so well encountered by such as I left for the guard of the Pale, as well of the army as of the country, led and commanded by the valiant knights Sir Warham St Leger[16] and Sir Nicholas Heron,[17] as with the loss of many of his horses and some of his men, he was driven home. And when he heard that I held my journey to Connacht, and was in the same, with all his force he approached the fort of the Derry, out of which the hardy Colonel Randolph issued, and gave him battle, and most nobly brake his battle, chased his horsemen and killed his footmen, until he [Randolph] charging where he saw the troop thickest, and leading more forwardly than readily followed, was overthrown and slain; whose fall saved many of the rebels' lives, for while the soldiers sought to rescue his lifeless body, they had leisure to run away. Yet the rebel lost the most of his best footmen, as well galloglas as shot, and many of his Scots for that day's work left his service, and no man of the garrison died that day but the colonel himself, though very many hurt who after recovered.

The rebel thus escaping by flight with his horsemen invaded further into O'Donnell's country, where he was so manfully met with by the good knight Sir Hugh O'Donnell, lately then, and yet is, captain of his country, as he was broken, with the slaughter of many of his principal horsemen, and the rest driven for safeguard of their lives to take the great water of Logh Swyllie, where the most of them, man or horse, were drowned.[18]

Seeing these good adventures achieved by others, I being absent from them, thought I would not be idle, for between the end of November and the beginning of Lent following I made many incursions into his country, sometimes as low as Dungannon, and with such diligence as my vauntcurrers [advance guard] have sworn to me that they have felt his couch warm where he lay that night, and yet their luck not to light on him.

In the Christmas holidays I visited him in the heart of his country, where he had made as great an assembly as he could, and had provided as great and good cheer as was to be had in the country, and when word was brought him that I was so near him, 'that is not possible,' quoth he, 'for the day before yesterday I know he dined and sate under his cloth of estate in the hall of Kilmaynham'. 'By O'Neill's hand!' quoth the messenger, 'he is in this country, and not far off, for I saw the red bracklok with the knotty club, and that is carried before none but himself' — meaning my pensel with the ragged staff.[19] With that he ran away, and so I shortened his Christmas, and made an end of mine own with abundance of his good provision, but not provided for such an unbidden guest as I was. So had I plagued him by that time as he was fully resolved to submit himself simply to me. And had I not dislodged, at the ordinary hour in camp to go to rest, with intent to do some exploit upon a great lym [*limb*, but possibly *lyme* as in *lyme-hound*: bloodhound] of his, he had come to me the next morning, but fearing the fury of the watch he durst not that night. This I think was the eighth or ninth road I made upon him, encamping sometime two, sometime three or four nights in his country; and how pleasant a life it is that time of the year, with hunger, and after sore travail to harbour long and cold nights in cabins made of boughs, and covered with grass, I leave to your indifferent judgement; thus and by these means I brought him very low.

But Sir — *Diabolus nunquam dormit*,[20] for now the Earl of Ormond[21] applied the Queen with such complaints against me and Sir Warham St Leger, whom I placed with others in commission in Munster, and her Majesty wrote so oft and earnestly to me by the procurement of the Earl of Ormond, touching hurts done to him and his by the Earl of Desmond,[22] as I was forced to leave my northern actions against O'Neill, and address me southward against Desmond, which prolonged the life and wars of O'Neill, greatly to the queen's charge.

So advanced I towards Munster in January, and came not home till April, not the pleasantest season of the year to make so long a journey in. The Earl of Desmond met me at Carrick (a house of Ormond's), whom I carried with me to Waterford, Dungarvan, Youghal and Cork; all the way hearing and ordering the complaints between the two earls. When the earl found that I dealt justly with Ormond, and that I rather showed favour than severity (as indeed I did to all his) after sundry and several speeches of very hard digestion, expressing his malicious intention, he would have been gone from me, which I denied him, and unwitting to him, appointed a guard to attend him day and night. I ordered against him a great sum, in recompense of damages done Ormond, and so took him with me to Kilmallock.

Then I was informed by his own brother, John,[23] and by [Hugh] Lacy, then bishop of Limerick, that he intended by force to rescue himself from me, and to that end had a great number of men in a readiness. Hereupon calling such noble men and potentates of Munster as I had with me, namely the Viscounts Barry and Roche, MacCarthy Reagh, Sir Dermod MacTeage [MacCarthy] of Muskrye, the barons Courcy and Lixnaw, with Condon, and a few other principal gentlemen of that province. I declared unto them what intelligence I had of Desmond's intention, and asked them whether they would give me their faithful promise and oath to take my part, and do as I would; for Desmond (said I) will I take, and as a prisoner lead away with me. They forthwith answered me as it were with one voice that they would to the uttermost adventure of their lives do whatsoever I would have them; thereupon I took such security of them as I thought convenient, and was indeed sufficient, and immediately sent for the Earl of Desmond, whom, in the presence of the forenamed personages, and the sovereign [mayor] of Kilmallock, with the best of his brethren of the same town, I did arrest, and committed him to the custody of my marshal, which arrest and commitment humbly upon his knees he yielded unto.

Then came to me the lords and others above written, and some captains whom I had in my company, and persuaded me that it was no policy, nor safe for me, to lead him out of that town, till I had greater force with me of such as I might trust. The noble men and others had none with them but their own menial train, which was not many. I had not, beside mine own household, but fifty English spears, fifty English shot, and fifty galloglas; these footmen I always kept about me in my journey as my guard. Much persuasion was made to me that I should not leave the town until I had gotten greater strength about me; but I seeing the town to be great and weak, and in many places easy to be scaled, sent to the mayor of Limerick, willing him to make ready for me as many men as he could, in warlike manner, well appointed, with all diligence to come to me, which he accomplished in such sort as (my letters being delivered unto him at eight of the clock in the afternoon) he advanced forth out of the gates of Limerick by one of the clock in the morning, three hundred well-appointed fighting men, who met me in the midway between Kilmallock and Limerick, the place appointed of meeting. Kilmallock is from Limerick twelve English miles. Out of that town I took a hundred and fifty men such as they were, appointed as well as it would be with them, and the rest above written. I issued out of the town of Kilmallock; but still came threatenings to me that I should be fought with by the way, and the prisoner taken from me, but I rested resolute that I would to Limerick, and lead Desmond prisoner with me, and protested to him in the hearing of a multitude that if the least violence that might be were offered to the basest churl or horse-boy of my train, he should die of my hand. And so mounting him on a worse horse than I rid on, marched away with him to Limerick; where after very few days I condemned him in the forfeiture of his bond to the Queen's majesty's use, for breach of the peace against the Earl of Ormond, of £20,000, and had him indicted according to form and order of law, for levying unlawfully men in warlike manner against me, her majesty's deputy, which is treason.

Here I constituted John of Desmond, his brother, to be seneschal and captain of all the earl's lands and seigniories, with charge and oath for his loyalty, and that he should, with all the speed he might, restore or recompense all her Majesty's subjects, who[m] Desmond had (I now remember not in how many years before) spoiled or injured; and so, making him knight, departed that city, leaving him behind, and still leading his brother prisoner with me. Sir John did so effectually in that his charge, as within three months after, I received letters of good credit that he had caused restitution to be made to the Queen's good subjects, oppressed by his brother's tyranny, of above five thousand pounds. These my acts (good Mr Secretary) are both registered and enrolled.

Then went I into and through the great countries of Thomond, and quieted all controversies in the same; I made the people apt to have and to obey a president and council, like as I had planted in Munster; I took pledges of all such as I thought necessary to take pledges of, and so (having the Earl of Thomond[24] with me) I passed through O'Shaughnessy's country, and came to Galway in Connacht, where I quieted and appeased sundry griefs and controversies between the Earl of Clanrickard[25] and other landlords of that province of Connacht. From thence I went through the same province to Athlone, where I found every thing in good quiet, in sort as I had left it in my former journey.

But all this my doing for the Earl of Ormond and his could nothing satisfy him, but still he exclaimed in England that he could have no justice of me, nor of the commissioners established in Munster, who were Sir Warham St Leger, the second baron of the exchequer, called [Robert] Cusake and Nicholas White, now master of the rolls in Ireland.[26] For Sir Warham St Leger I do know him for a worthy honest gentleman, and one that would not blemish his credit for either of both the earls. Cusake I deemed to be more affected to Desmond than Ormond, White I knew, and all others that knew him thought him to be affectiously devoted to Ormond, as one born his follower, and yet both honest.

This composition of a Council I thought convenient, for the primitive reformation of so old a cancered faction as was and yet is between the two earls, who albeit they would inveigh each against other, yet if any sentence passed for the advancement of the Queen's prerogative, or suppression of either of their tyrannies, straightways it was cried out of, and complained of to the Queen, specially by the Earl of Ormond, as injustice and oppression. And thereupon received I many a bitter letter, which indeed tired me, and so perplexed my most dear wife, as she fell most grievously sick upon the same, and in that sickness remained once in trance above fifty-two hours! Upon whose recovery I sent her into England, where she lived till my coming over, somewhat to my charges.

But now again to my story. Leaving Thomond and Connacht in good order and quiet, with a short refreshing of me and my men at home, I addressed myself northward, to the prosecution of my former wars against the arch-rebel Shane O'Neill, whom I found, by reason of the former reported intermission, procured by the Earl of Ormond (upon what conceit I know not, or at least will not judge) to have gotten breath again, and of much more strength, as well of Scots as Irish, than I left of in January last before, when I advanced southward. And now was it the end of April, when I eftsoons renewed my wars with him. I placed myself and my forces as near him as I could conveniently, and made as many invasions upon him as my men's bodies and horses might endure, I thank Almighty God very little or nothing to our loss, and to his and his country's utter waste and ruin. He (no longer being able to make men of his own, to make head against the smallest foray that I could send into his country) practised with Alaster Oge MacDonnell, an Irish Scot, and among them a grand captain, to serve him;[27] but as I writ to you before, upon the battle fought at the fort of Derry, the most of his mercenary Scots left him, with whom and among the rest, this Alaster Oge was one.

The honest, valiant and politique Captain Piers,[28] being before made by me seneschal of Clandeboy, according to my direction did deal so as the traitor's practice by some providence was prevented; and whereas he looked for service at their hands against me, for service of me they killed him the 22nd day of June, and I began my wars with him the 22nd day of September before; so the wars endured eight months (whereof three I spent in Munster about the Earl of Ormond's causes as above rehearsed) and sent me his head pickled in a pipkin, and craved their reward, and (as I think if they be not lately satisfied) they do so still, as I know, not many years since, in your presence, at the Council board the forenamed Alaster Oge did by his letters, and Captain Piers.[29]

Thus had I that unnatural monster's head, but then I did and yet do fear that the old cancered body whereof sometime it was head, I mean the lineage and surname of the O'Neills, will breed (*Hydra fashion*) more heads, and haply as ill or worse than he. Of this good success I advertised her majesty and the lords of the privy council, and immediately (calling to me the most part of the nobility of the English Pale, and the counsellors of that estate) with the army I went down into Ulster, as far as the great water called by some the Black Water. There (lying in camp) I had yielded unto me all holds or fast places that Shane O'Neill kept anything of price in; more specially the pledges or prisoners (amongst whom was Thomas Vaughan, an honest valiant gentleman, and lieutenant of a company of horsemen) which he had taken, and did keep of other landlords his neighbours, or his own not the best trusted followers. Which pledges through hard keeping and famine were in most pitiful and miserable case. Among those places that were delivered me, an island (standing in Lough Neagh, by the country, now called Island Sydney [Island Magee], which place Shane thought to be of most strength of any that he had, and where he kept his plate, jewels and apparel) was one.

To my camp there came Turlo Lenough [Turlough Luineach O'Neill], who had been in Shane's life tanist of Tyrone, and yet by me made in these wars his enemy.[30] He was by the people of that country chosen O'Neill, which title in truth he accepted, being given him with the brutish ceremonies incident to the same. There came with him the principallest of all his surname, and I had with me the young baron of Dungannon, Shane's eldest brother's son, whom I had bred in my house from a little boy, then very poor of goods, and full feebly friended.[31] I then (in the presence and hearing of all that were in my camp, as well of them who came with me, as those that came with him, and all other the potentates and landlords of Ulster, rebuked him sharply for taking upon him the title of O'Neill afore Her Majesty's pleasure were known, affirming unto him that I would not confirm the same, but would write to her Highness to nobilitate him, with title and degree of higher honour and dignity, which he seemed reverently to accept and willingly to expect her Majesty's resolution. I then set down in form of articles certain covenants briefly, and (as far as I can remember) these as follows.[32] That he should not take upon him the name of O'Neill till Her Majesty's pleasure were known; that he should disclaim any superiority, rent or service taken before by Shane, or any of his ancestors, over or of any of those landlords which were commonly termed his uriaghes, the which are before recited, and that he should cease to exact other rent or service, or other buying (as they call it there) of the country called the Route, or MacGwillin's [*MacQuillan's*] country, which descended of the Welsh name Llewelin[33] nor of the Glens, then and now possessed by Scots, but of right ought to have been the lands of the Barons Missett [*recte* Bisset], being English; nor of Clandeboy, the lands of a lineage of the O'Neills; nor of the two Ards, the more and less, being the possession of the Lord Savage and other gentlemen and freeholders of English surname; nor of the country of Lecale, the possessions of the Earl of Kildare, Russell, and other gentlemen of English race; nor of the Dufferin, being the lands of the Whites, an English lineage; nor of the lands of the late abbey of the Newry; nor of the lordship of Mourne and Green Castle; nor of the lordship of Cowle, Carlingford and Omath, being the lands and possessions of Sir Nicholas Bagenal, knight; nor entertain any Scots, either borne in the Glens or in Scotland, without special licence of the governor for the time being.

Then I descended with him into the consideration of his own country of Tyrone, meaning indeed the dissipation of the same; and appointed unto him all the lands beneath or by north the Blackwater, with the service of O'Kane, MacCann, O'Donnelly, O'Quinn, and two other landlords of like rank as the meanest of the last beforenamed, whose names I have now forgotten; and to bear the title of principal of his surname. I appointed unto Turlo Brasylogh [*Turlough Brasselagh*] the lands called Clanbrassil; this Turlo was the son of the eldest son of Con, first Earl of Tyrone.[34] Then allotted I to Hugh, baron of Dungannon, and of right ought to be Earl of Tyrone, all the lands called the O'Neill's lands, the very first and most ancient possession of the O'Neills, lying above and by south the greatwater [Blackwater]. I exempted him from taking any exaction upon any of the lands of the church of Armagh, or any member of the same; to all which covenants he agreed, to the great rejoicing and contentment of all the proprietors of that province.[35] Saving some particular and peculiar followers of his own, who much repined that the great and regal estate of the O'Neill (as they deemed it) should be so broken and dismembered.

Then dealt I with O'Donnell and with Con, who both were in my camp; which Con was eldest son to Callogh, eldest brother unto Hugh then and now O'Donnell, at that time lately dead, and nephew to Turlo Lenogh.[36] This Con looked to be captain of the country, but the bishops and other landlords of the same elected Sir Hugh to be O'Donnell. Whereupon there was great likelihood of great wars, which I quieted, establishing Hugh in the place of O'Donnell, and gave unto Con the castles of Liffar [Ir. *Leifear*: Lifford] and Finn, and the lands belonging to the same, being a good third part of all Tirconnell. I planted three garrisons in Clandeboy and the Glens, namely the good old Captain William Piers, with a company of footmen, in the castle and town of Carrickfergus; the renowned soldier Captain Malby with a company of horsemen in Belfast; and the lusty young Captain William Horsey in Glenarm in the Glens; and a ward in Island Sydney under James Vaughan; lastly I made Alastair Oge and all his Scots who killed Shane, and all other Scots not born in Ireland to depart the realm, and the rest born in Ireland and inhabiting the Glens offered to hold that country of her majesty by rent and service.*

All these things being agreed upon, engrossed, signed, sealed and delivered, I thought I had done a good work to my sovereign and country, and to the people of that land. And sure in a good hour it was done, for it has continued ever since, and each landlord enjoys that possession I left him in, saving McGuire, whom the Earl of Essex[37] when he was General of Ulster gave to O'Neill, to hold of him by rent and service, as Shane before had challenged in the time of the deputation of Sir William Fitzwilliam,[38] which in my opinion was not well done. And

---

* Marginal note in another hand: 'Sir Henry Sidney caused the Scots men born in Ireland to hold of the Queen of England by rent assured in 1582.'

thus leaving all parties as they seemed well contented, and they and the whole province generally in quiet, I returned to Dublin, where I caused these my acts to be registered and enrolled, and so I suppose they remain of record at this day.*

But there I heard that the Earl of Ormond ceased not to persecute me with unjust and untrue informations, alleging that his people could have no justice, but were still oppressed by Sir John of Desmond and the Desmonians. And hearing also that it was resolved that for saving of charges, that I should abate my forces, and should not proceed in building of bridges, towns and forts, when (in all true policy and expedience) more charges should have been bestowed not only upon the works last beforenamed, but likewise upon introduction of colonies of English and other loyal subjects, whereby a perpetual inhabitation would have ensued, to the recompense as well of that which was spent, as for a yearly and continual profit by rent and service, and strength of the country against all foreign invasion. I then procured my revocation, being tired in body with my long and most painful travail: but more wearied in mind, with the sharp and bitter letters which I almost weekly received out of England by the procurement of the Earl of Ormond, condemning me for every thing that was amiss in Munster, though I never so much busied nor sped so well in Ulster, and obtained the same with great satisfaction and joy for my victory of [sic] such an Arch-Rebel and other my good adventures, and passed the seas attended on by O'Connor Sligo, captain of his country called Carbery, O'Carroll, captain of his country called Ely O'Carroll, the baron of Dungannon, Patrick FitzMaurice, eldest son of [Thomas FitzMaurice] the baron of Lixnaw, John O'Reilly, eldest son to [Hugh] O'Reilly, a great man, and of the province of Connacht anciently, but adjoining to the English Pale, captain of the country called Breni [*Breifne*] O'Reilly; and Ross Magochigan [*MacGeoghegan*], eldest son to [Connla] Magochigan, captain of his country called Kynaliagh [*Kinelagh*]. All these and many others went with me at their own suit, chiefly to behold the high

---

* Marginal note: 'At this time I caused the old ruinous castle of Dublin to be re-edified, and therein to be made the best lodging for the governor that is in Ireland.'

majesty of our sacred Sovereign, and also in their own behalf and their fathers to surrender unto her Highness's hands all their lands, seigniories, and titles to lands, for all which they had yielded to the crown nothing, or some small service, and to receive the same again of her, yielding far more greater rent and service. And received their lands and other her majesty's graces most bountifully, as by sundry and several letters doth appear.[39]

But when I came to the court it was told me it was no war that I had made, nor worthy to be called a war, for that Shane O'Neill was but a beggar, an outlaw, and one of no force; and that the Scots stumbled on him by chance. But such a beggar he was that after a former war made in the government of the Earl of Sussex a peace was made with him, not the most honourablest, and as he and his would say, he was entreated to come into England, and there rewarded of her majesty with fair and good apparel, and £2,500 lent him, but as he termed, given him to buy his peace. Sure I am the money he had, the apparel and other gifts, and nothing had ever the Queen for it again, saving his head. This may argue he was no beggar.

And within few days after, I was charged for not redressing the damages done to Ormond and his followers by Sir John of Desmond, whom I left seneschal and captain of his brother's country, as before is mentioned, his brother still remaining with me in captivity. And there it was openly spoken, that the Butlers could have no justice against Sir John of Desmond neither by Sidney or St Leger, whom I had left chief in commission to minister justice in Munster, and unwitting to me the Earl of Desmond and Sir John, his brother, were sent for; which Sir John (being come to Dublin for conference with the lords justices, was (together with his brother the earl) sent as prisoners and committed to the Tower of London, where they remained, I think, seven years after; and truly Mr Secretary this hard dealing with Sir John of Desmond was the origin of James FitzMaurice's rebellion, and consequently of all the evil and mischief in Munster, which since (I can prove) has cost the crown of England and that country a hundred thousand pounds. When they were come, I was eftsoons charged with partiality between the earls, and in especial for what I did not apprehend them sooner than I did. For the younger brother I had no warrant, nor (in truth) saw no cause, but much to the contrary; and for the other I was driven to prove that I had apprehended him and committed prisoner in Kilmallock (as afore is mentioned) forty-eight days before the letter was written at St James for to apprehend him. Thus have you (my dear sir) some declaration of my painful travail, good event, and victory in this my first deputation; but of reward I can say no more but as he did who said — *foris triumpho at domi plero*.[40]

But now (Sir) according to my former presage, the late beheaded *Hydra* began to bud forth a new head; for Turlo Lenogh seeing no plantation to follow after so great a destruction of the people of Tyrone, nor garrisons maintained, but diminished, or totally withdrawn, grew proud and insolent, and demanded and arrogated his ancient truage [*trewage*: tribute] and service of his uriaghes by poll (as you have heard) renounced; which being advertised into England, I was not six months at home, but I was sent for to attend the court about Irish causes, and dismissed again; and yet again sent for, and again I am sure three or four several times, not a little to my charges. For as the people of that country were desirous to have me, so was there some of this country unwilling that I should go; yet at the last, before a full year was run out, I was sent again deputy into Ireland. And for that the first service seemed most necessary to be done in the north, I directed my course that way, and landed at Carrickfergus, the 6th day of September 1568.

Turlo Lenogh hearing of my landing there, came to Bann side to a place where the same river issues out of the great Logh; with him I used such interparlance as he was contented to cease from challenging any more the oft remembered uriaghes, and promised me faithfully when his wife[41] returned out of Scotland he would come to me into some more convenient place of meeting than that was, which he performed. Thereupon some order being taken with the McQuillans and the native Scots of Ireland inhabiting the two countries of Route and Glens, I returned to Carrickfergus, where I found the garrisons I there left (as is before mentioned) in the latter end of my former deputation, in very good order, as well for the obedience of the people to serve them as to furnish them with victuals; for they would rise out with them in hostile manner as oft as the captains would command them. And their victual was at very easy price, as a fat cow at 6s 8d, and 24 eggs for a penny, and so every thing mean between the egg and the beef was sold at like rate. And this not only for the soldiers but likewise for the deputy and captains' houses; and surely, sir, so it might have been kept, if the violent and intempestyne proceeding of the Earl of Essex and his followers had not been; for undoubtedly if the treasure, horses, victuals and other furniture, as well for the war as husbandry, which was spent and spoiled in that his enterprise, whereof came no good, but the destruction of that town, with the church, and utter ruin of all the country about, had been well employed, and seasons of the year observed, and leisure taken in dealing with the people, had been sufficient to have reduced all the last forenamed countries to as good obedience as the English Pale, and to have walled and made Carrickfergus a good and strong town; in which there was twice a week a good market kept, where not only all kinds of things of that country breed was to be sold, but out of the English Pale, the Isle of Man and Scotland came much merchandise, victuals and other commodities, and out of France in one summer three barks of forty tonnes apiece discharged their loading of excellent good Gascoigne wine, the which they sold for nineteen cow skins the hogshead.

While I lay thus in that town I surveyed and viewed by myself and others the county of whole Clandeboy and Ards, and shired the same by the name of the county of Carrickfergus, and whether I put the Glens into the same or not in truth I have forgotten. The country (Sir) was in such quiet as the captains and soldiers would as ordinarily hunt and take others their pleasures as if they had lain in the English Pale; for at my arrival the archbishop of Armagh [Thomas Lancaster] and the bishop of Meath [Hugh Brady], with divers noblemen and gentlemen as well of England and the English Pale, lawyers, merchants and others came from Dublin to Carrickfergus only for visitation sake (the bishops riding in their rochets [surplices] and the rest unarmed). Thus

Narrative

the town and country set in good order as I thought, I journeyed towards Dublin, and (being fain to keep the fields for lack of houses to lie in) wanted not, wheresoever I lodged, anything that country had, in abundance brought in by the people thereof, and as it seemed, with hearty good will. By the way there met me all the horsemen and freeholders of the Ards, Magennis, the captain of Kylultagh, the captain of Kylwarlyn [*Culverin*].[42]

And so dismissing the horsemen and footmen of Clandeboy, with easy journey I came to Dublin, where I had not been but a while, but that James FitzMaurice,[43] son to Maurice of Desmond, nicknamed Attotane, brother to James [14th Earl of Desmond], (father to the now earl, traitor and rebel), understanding that I was arrived and had not brought with me neither the earl nor Sir John, his brother, which he thought I might and would have done, assembling as many of the Earl of Desmond's people as he could, declared unto them, that I could not obtain the enlargement either of the earl or his brother John, and there was no hope or expectation of either of them but to be put to death or condemned to perpetual prison. And therefore (seeing that the country could not be without an earl or a captain) willed them to make choice of one to be their earl or captain, as their ancestors had done, after the murder (as he termed it) of the good earl Thomas FitzJames, his ancestor, put to death by the tyrant the Earl of Worcester, as he called him, then Deputy of Ireland, and according to this his speech he wrote unto me.[44]

They forthwith, and as it had been with one voice, cried him to be their captain, and him they vowed to follow and obey his commandment; and by and by he assembled forces, not much extraordinary, but full as much as it had been accustomed by any earl or captain, which was by me forbidden, and accordingly forborne by Sir John of Desmond. Upon consideration of his letter and other advertisement of his doings, I writ unto him, and used all other the best mediation I could that he should desist from that unlawful usurpation. He answered me frivolously, then used I threats; but all that I could do would not serve, but the more I writ the worse he did, and persisted still in assembling of men of war, to the great annoyance and burden of the people of his own country and neighbours, whereof they grievously complained, but I by no means could redress it.

Here may you (Sir) as I writ before, see the origin of the rebellion in Munster, which never since could be so totally quenched, but either in action or intention it had life; and, to use plain terms, it was the withdrawing of Sir John of Desmond from the governing of that country, where he governed well, and the long imprisonment of him, which was the Earl of Ormond's counsel, and lastly the enlargement of them both; for if the one had been kept, though the other enlarged, each had been a sufficient hostage upon the other. James grew into more and more insolencies and great outrages upon divers whom he loved nor liked not; whereupon I was driven to proclaim him traitor and rebel. And looking for the service of Sir Edmund Butler,[45] then captain and seneschal of the Earl of Ormond's countries (for so the earl his brother had made him, and politiquely kept himself in England, as well for duty's sake to the Queen as ancient and innate malice to the Earl of Desmond and all Desmonians), I was quite disappointed, being answered as well by scornful letters as frivolous and foolish speeches, that he was able to do none, alleging that I had made him to ride up and down the country like a priest, inferring thereby the suppressing of the most filthy and intolerable exaction of coyne and livery, used most harmfully by him, the country being quiet, and as wars not likely to be. I urging him still to serve, he fell into rebellious actions, for he wasted and destroyed almost all the Queen's County, killing very many of the inhabitants of the same, but most specially all the Englishmen, and for more despite to the action, he would cause English dead men's bodies to be stripped out of their English garments and their hose and doublets (being stuffed and trussed) he would set up as marks for his kernes to throw their darts at. He wasted much of the county of Carlow, and of the Kavenaghs as many as would not be of his rebellious faction.

He did much hurt in the bounds of the counties of Dublin and Kildare; he utterly spoiled a great fair held at Inyscorthie [*Enniscorthy*], a house and town of the Queen's in the county of Washford [*Wexford*]. I am sure that fair is far the greatest of any in Ireland, and held yearly, and usually at a day certain. The horrible rapes, the shameful murders, with the total rapine of all the goods that could be carried away, were too loathsome to be written or read. There were assembled (beside a multitude of country people) the most of the merchants of the good town of Washford, either in their own persons, their wives or their servants, who were ravished, killed or spoiled, all looking for no such an unheard of harm there, whither peaceably they came by water.

Then increased he his strength by stirring the Earl of Thomond to rebellion, and to resist Sir Edward Fitton, then lord president in Connacht and Thomond;[46] and had with him both his brethren Edward and Piers, the sons of the Viscount of Mountgarret, his uncle, and by far the most part of all the fighting men of both the counties of Tipperary and Kilkenny; for although some householders and principal gentlemen, more wary than the rest, went not, their sons, servants and followers (as they term them there) went to him. And finally all the Ormonists of what surname soever they were, except Sir Theobald Butler, lord of the Kaer [*Cahir*], and the Lord [James] Butler of Dunboyne's people (who then was in England, and under age) rebelled with him. James FitzMaurice for his part had gotten to him the Earl of Clancare [Donal MacCarthy More],[47] McDonough, McAuley, O'Keeffe, O'Suillivan Moore, and I think O'Suillivan Bere, joined with him; and though the rest of the potentates of Munster remained (or they seemed) sound, yet their young and loose people went to him; and for that so virtuous an action as this rebellion was, might be of more strength, but Butler and Garadyne [*Geraldine*], notwithstanding all former and most ancient enmities, joined together, and spoiled those that would not go with them, at their pleasures. I sent the good knight Sir Peter Carew[48] and the valiant Malby, to keep the frontiers of Carlow and the Cavanaghs' country; and the hardy and politique Captain [William] Collier into the good town of Kilkenny, the people whereof I did not very soundly trust. Sir Peter Carew and Captain Malby gave Sir Edmund Butler a shrewd blow after a bloody bickering and slaughter of his men and chased him, won his house at Cloghgrennan, and hanged the ward. Sir Edmund returning to James FitzMaurice, they both with their forces encamped and besieged the town of Kilkenny, where the earl his brother has strong castle, and the town is well closed and defended with gates, walls and river; but had not the soldiers been, the town had been sacked, and many of the people ransomed, as I after in truth found; but Captain Collier so vigilantly attended his charge, as well in guarding the gates and walls against the rebels as in preventing the practice of the townsmen, as the rebels were forced to go away with shame; against whom I advanced with as much diligence as I could, leading only with me the garrison men, which were but 600, leaving all the men of the country to guard the Pale northward, and Sir Barnaby FitzPatrick to guard the Pale southward, who was the most sufficient man in counsel and action for the war that ever I found of that country birth, great pity it was of his death.[49]

I came to Kilkenny, where after [I] had allowed of some with thanks, and checked others with rebukes, I marched into the county of Tipperary, where the rebels were before me, burning their own houses and villages. Some of their castles I won, but so many as I would I could not tarry about to win, for that I daily was advertised of the great distress the city of Cork was in, where at that time lay a full noble and virtuous lady, [Ursula] the wife of Sir Warham St Leger, whom the citizens were sometimes in consultation and consideration to deliver to James FitzMaurice, which he earnestly, and with great threats required.[50] For whose rescue I sent forth a ship furnished with mine own menial servants and others, who by reason of contrary wind could not come thither in due time; but there arrived in very good season (so directed by me) 400 footmen sent with great diligence out of England, led by Captain [John] Sute and Captain [John] Ward, two very sufficient men, whose coming not only comforted the poor desolate lady, but the whole city before sore afraid.

So marching through the county of Tipperary, I encamped by Clonmel, a walled town standing upon the river of Suir, the people good and loyal. During my encamping there, the rebels being dispersed all over the country, there was libells and chartells [leaflets] thrown into my camp, signifying that I should not so soon dislodge but that I should be fought withal; yea and peradventure in my camp itself. I sent to the mayor and his brethren of Waterford to send me some relief of men furnished for the war. They flatly answered me they would send none; albeit some particular men, namely Piers Aylward, who had been mayor of Waterford, John Wyse and Anthony Poore [Power] and some others very well appointed, of their own good wills came to me, offering their service, with the adventure of their lives in that action. There came also to me certain seamen, and they were tall fellows led by a good soldier and tall gentleman called Marshall, servant to my Lord of Warwick, and offered me their service, whereof I was right glad, and in truth they did me good service; and here I think worthy to be noted the refusal of the city of Waterford, alleging they might so do by point and grant of their charter, for that over-large grants to such corporations are dangerous; but at my coming home I made their corporation well pay for it, as Mr Tremayne, who served me then as Secretary, if he be alive can well testify.[51]

Here I sent forth proclamations of pardon to all such as would desist from rebellion (certain exempted) but it prevailed not. I sent also commissioners to parley with the principal gentlemen of the county of Tipperary, to dissuade them from that furious, unnatural and traitorous action they were in, but nothing took place; the gentlemen answering thus as follows: 'We are of this county more ancient inhabiters and freeholders than any Butler is, and were the first conquerors of this soil from the Irishry; and in our ancestors' days it was made of a county called Earthmound[52] (as much to say as East Munster) but since that time (though a good many years past) England gave us away' (I use their own phrase) 'to a Butler, and created him Earl of Ormond, made him by letters patent lord of the Liberty of the county of Tipperary, where, as a County Palatine, he keeps courts regally by himself or his officers, to which courts we do, and our ancestors did, ever since the grant from the King of England, yield suit and service, and where all actions for goods, lands or life are tried, very few except, and those being but four capital offences, seldom or never committed here. And thus have we and our ancestors acknowledged him as our lord and captain, and indeed know no other sovereign but him, whose lieutenant Sir Edmund Butler, his brother and heir apparent, is; him we follow, and him we will follow, and do as he commands us.' That was all I could get of them.

And Sir Edmund Butler being demanded (for so I was directed out of England that he should be) what the cause was that he rebelled, he said it was my hard dealing with him; — 'Wherein?', said he that examined him. 'Marry,' quoth Sir Edmund, 'openly in the Star Chamber he said that he would sit on my skirts; and that hereafter came not yet; and that he would make my heartstrings ache'—where in truth (Sir) I used no such words to him nor to any, nor they were not, nor are not, any phrases of mine. He alleged them to be spoken in the Star Chamber, on a court day, the chamber was full, the court was furnished with lords, bishops and counsellors. I asked of them and of many other plain and honest gentlemen, whether any such words had passed me or no; they all affirmed that neither those words nor any the like were spoken by me. Indeed he was there before me to answer to sundry his outrageous acts rebuked by me, and whether committed or no, truly I have forgotten. To his complices in rebellion he would say that the cause of his stir was, that the Earl of Leicester, enemy to his brother and house, should marry the queen, and be king of England, and that I should be king of Ireland; their mortal foe and brother to the Earl of Leicester, of whom I should hold Ireland (as might appear) by bearing the ragged staff continually in my pensil before me, which indeed I did.[53] This did the Earl of Clancare[54] and others tell me that he said unto them; and lastly, that blessed babe, Edward Butler,[55] a page of my own bringing up, talking with some servants of mine, his old and familiar fellows, whom of purpose I sent with the commissioners to understand of him what they could, for they were well acquainted with the young man's humour; and he (pretending great good will and love to me, for the sundry benefits and favours he had received of me) wished them and prayed them, even with tears, that they would persuade me to return back, affirming that if I went forwards, I was but undone, for overthrown I should be, naming who and whose men they had in their company, and ready at their call when they would, and said they were I cannot tell how many thousand. But I think the gentleman (not greatly expert in arithmetic) added a cipher or two too many; and said to one or two (of his most familiars) of my folks that he nor they did anything without the privity and direction of the Earl of Ormond, then in England.

When my commissioners were returned and brought no submission from the rebels, but report of their insolent arrogance, and that it was known that the city of Waterford had refused to send me any succours of men, and the libells daily scattered in my camp importing great threats and scorn of me and my small company, and extolling their own mighty forces, with news of arrival of foreign enemies, as it made such an impression of fear in my men's hearts as it was most strange for me to behold. For I might see by the very countenances of as resolute men as any I had, wonderful alteration; for the private soldiers came to their officers, the officers to their captains, the captains to my counsellors, and the counsellors to me, and nothing in their mouths but 'home! home! home! or else we were all undone'; so mighty were the rebels; so tickle was the English Pale; so strong was Turlo Lenough, and so small a company were we.

I hearing of this, sent for the council and captains into my tent, and had some conference with them; all which, saving two, persuaded me to return, affirming they found great faintness in the soldiers. But I somewhat replying and showing my disposition to go forwards, Sir Thomas Cusake[56] and Sir Lucas Dillon,[57] but especially that good knight Sir Lucas, animated me to go forwards, reviling the villainy of the rebels, and assuring the sufficiency of the army, if they would do their devoir [duty], though it were but small. These two gentlemen accompanied me from the beginning of the journey to the end of the same, and in truth (Sir) they did the Queen excellent and beneficial service, but chiefly Sir Lucas, and, by the way, I upon my credit and knowledge affirm that the Queen has not so sufficient a counsellor of that country's birth, nor no prince a more faithful and loyal a servant and subject, of what nation soever he be, as well it has appeared by his counsel and action, as well in the time of my government as since.

This wearisome consultation being interrupted by me, out of my pavilion I went into the market place of my camp, and with trumpet and drum sounded to the standard, the soldiers and all the rest of the camp readily came, in hope that I would forthwith have returned; I showed my resolution to the contrary, and some words I spoke, and somewhat it prevailed; for they with the drinking of a tun of wine, which during the consultation was provided and laid in the market place, and after my speech ended, very diligently applied both by drawing and drinking, all my men's cowardish coldness was turned into martial-like heat, and then nothing but 'Upon them! upon them! Lead you, and we will follow to the land's end, or die by the way; and let us go by and by.' 'Nay, soft sirs,' quoth I, 'it is Sunday, and it is afternoon, we will go and hear evening prayer, sup and rest, and you shall be called I warrant you, betimes in the morning, and so in the name of God we will advance forwards.'

That evening and all the night there was nothing but singing, casting of bullets, drying of powder, filing of pikes' heads, sharpening of swords, and every man thinking himself good enough for five rebels. The night seemed long to them, and as soon as it was day I dislodged, marching through sundry straits (there called fastness), advantageous enough for the rebels to have fought with me, but unfought withal, and without loss of any of my carriage (which I much doubted) and accordingly provided for; and without sight of any rebel that durst make head against any of my camp. I marched into the White Knight's country, a good and large tract of land; the name of the country I have forgotten, and many and strong castles in it. The owner of the country was in actual rebellion with James FitzMaurice, and not long after in his service slain.[58]

Here I left the Butlers' dominions, and entered into the Garadynes' [*Geraldines'*]; at the entry of which met me the Viscount Barry, the Viscount Roche, MacCarthy Reagh, and divers other gentlemen of the province of Munster, all pretending loyalty to the Queen, and enmity to the house of Desmond. I went to the principal castle of the White Knight's country, called the old or the new castle, I wot [know] not whether;[59] and summoned the ward by sound of trumpet, who answered they held that castle of none but God, James FitzMaurice and the White Knight; and unless one of them would come (or send St Peter or St Paul), they would never render it; with other scornful spiteful speeches. I was persuaded by the forenamed noblemen that the house was very strong, well furnished with men, powder and small shot; well barbicaned I saw it was, and well flanked; and [they] advised me to leave it unattempted and pass by. But being advertised of the arrival of the above-written captains and soldiers in Cork, I determined to win it ere I went, and encamped very near it, and planted such artillery as I had, which was but a saker [a small cannon] and two minions [small pieces of ordnance], to it. Full lively my men went to work, and before night won the barbican; the next morning the artillery kept such play at the battlements and cage-work, and my small shot at their lopes [loopholes] and windows, as the pioneers made some way into the castle, most hazardously assaulting the same, where they were hard[i]ly resisted by the rebels. The house was vaulted with stone, so as fire could do them no hurt. Notwithstanding, the soldiers by fair force of fighting drove them up into the first and greatest vault, with the loss of a great many of their lives, and some hurt of themselves. So sped I upon them that whole day; in the night following I (tendering the lives of my men) sent to them to yield, offering them safety to go away. They answered me that they had promised James FitzMaurice to keep it for him, and he had promised them to rescue them if need were, which they looked for, and I might find ere many hours were past, little to my liking.

As soon as it was day I caused to sound to the assault, whereto my men went, and that so lustily as having made somewhat a larger passage than the stair, with sword and target they won the first vault, and killed a great many of the defenders; yet divers of them got up by other privy stairs unto the top of the castle, and into other rooms vaulted, whom my men never ceased to ferret out. Captain [William] Collier and Captain [Thomas] Cheston, who led them that day, and showed themselves very valorous men, told me that the rebels had made seven or eight fights after the first vault was won. Finally, with very small loss of my men, or hurt of the castle, I won the same, and left nothing alive in it; and delivering it to James Roche, son of the Viscount Roche, to be kept to her majesty's use, and sundry other castles and lands to Sir Theobald Butler, withheld from him by the White Knight, I dislodged and marched towards Cork. By the way no rebel resisted me, no castle held me out, but either they razed them and burnt them and ran away, or submitted them and their castles to me.

So (wasting and spoiling all that country) with as convenient speed as I could, I came to the city of Cork, where I found the above-written captains and soldiers. I in manner revived the poor afflicted lady and comforted the citizens of the same city. I there heard of the arrival of the Earl of Ormond, whom I addressed to meet me at Limerick; and after I had refreshed me and my men a few days, I departed from thence and encamped in a country of the Earl of Desmond's, called Kiriewherie [*Kerrycurrihy*], and destroyed the same, winning the principal castle thereof, called Carreg-Ilyn [*Carrigaline*], and left in it a ward.[60] From thence I marched into MacDonogh's country, which confines with Desmond [and] the Earl of Clancare's country; and there I won and pulled down castles, burned and spoiled villages and fields; which, while I was in doing, the lords of the country, O'Kueefe, MacAulley, the eldest son of O'Suillivan More (the father for age and corpulence not being able to travel), and O'Suillivan Bere, without protection came to me and submitted themselves, lives and lands; and there taking of them oath and hostage for their fidelity, without pardon, I dismissed them to expect the queen's mercy. I then turned into a great territory of land of the Viscount Barry's, the name of the country I have forgotten, but the principal castle thereof bears a French name called *Bowte de vawne* [*Buttevant*], which I took, and repossessed the right owner in it; so I did divers landlords and freeholders whose lands and castles had been taken and withheld from them, some of long time by the Earl of Desmond, and some of late time by James FitzMaurice.

Then and there I heard that the rebel James (with his associates) went afore me wasting and destroying the queen's good subjects, as well of the county of Cork as the county of Limerick, and therefore was constrained to alter my former intention of going into Desmond, and turned towards the county of Limerick; but I could not get so far as Killmallock but that the rebel had by scale surprised the same town, not without vehement suspicion of falsehood in many of the townsmen, for some he saved, many he sacked, some he ransomed, and many houses of base building he burned, which afterwards were re-edified, the walls heightened, and the town made better than ever it was.

Here I received answer from the Earl of Ormond that he could not come to me without convoy of good force to conduct him, protesting he could not command ten men in all his country, besides those his household servants, whom he had brought with him out of England, and were not many. I sent him the Viscount Decies,[61] a Garrandyne [*Geraldine*], but enemy to the Earl of Desmond, and the Lord Poer.[62] These two noblemen are great men in the county of Waterford, and the Earl of Ormond's cousins germain. These two noblemen I forgot to name before, but they had been in my camp ever since I departed from Clonmel.

They brought the earl to me safe (I lying in camp hard by the city of Limerick). The earl delivered me the queen's majesty's most honourable letters, containing most constant and confident opinion in his loyal devotion to her power and service, and exceeding and surpassing any prince's clemency, her inclination to have mercy on his brethren, the rebels. He besought me that he might work their retreat from their vile and most wilful actions. I required him so to do, which he promised effectually to go about to do, and before I removed he brought me his brother Edward, my late page, before somewhat remembered; and, coming into my camp, armed as well defensively as offensively, I disdained the same, and afore I would see him, made him to be disarmed. When he came to me, after some rigorous speeches used by me, he humbly submitted himself and confessed his fault, and I committed him to my marshal's ward.

The earl said that he would do his best to bring in his two other brethren, but I saw them not all that journey; and made most earnest suit to me that he might have his brother Edward in custody, affirming that he was more able to work with his other two brethren than he himself. I granted his request, and upon his bond, body for body, to have him further coming when he should be called (which I have yet to show), he carried him with him, and so departed from me; but since that time, during that my deputation, I could never set eye on mine old servant Edward.

During my abode in Limerick there came to me divers principal personages of the same county of Kerry, and of Conelogh [*Conello*: barony in Kerry regarded as a separate county for most of the period], as the Lord FitzMaurice, Sir William Burgh,[63] captain or owner of Clanwilliam, a man of great lands, whose eldest son after (being my man) with his own hand killed James FitzMaurice, and James him, at one only encounter; Lacy, Purcell and Suppell, with many more, whose names I have forgotten; being all descended of English race; all swore allegiance to her majesty, and faithful service in that action against James. There came to me also Rorie MacShee, captain-general of the Earl of Desmond's galloglas, surnamed Clanshee: he likewise submitted, swore loyalty, and delivered pledges as before. This man was counted one of much might among them; he procured to come to me a great many more of the Irishry.[64]

Thus having (as I thought) well plucked the principal feathers of James's wings, I redressed all the particular quarrels as well as I could, that there were between party and party, being good subjects. I saw Limerick and Kilmallock well furnished with men, munition and victual, and taking order for the victualling of the garrison there left, which was 200 footmen, led by Captain Sute, 200 footmen led by Captain Warde, and 100 horsemen led by Captain [Humphrey] Gilbert,[65] whom I constituted comander and colonel of those companies and of all Munster.

These gentlemen, captains and soldiers, did so diligently and valiantly their devoir, as they brought James FitzMaurice to a very base estate; he made many skirmishes with him, and always prevailed; he pulled from him so many of his men, besides those he killed, as he made him very feeble. So, enjoying great victory of the suppressed rebel, he [Gilbert] came to me with great joy to Tredath [*Drogheda*], bringing with him sundry personages of good account; some such as I had not dealt withal at my being at Cork or Limerick. And expecting for the same to have received triumph in England, untimely he desired leave to go thither, and unseasonably, after that I had made him knight, I granted him so to do. For after his departure the rebel got force again, though confronted with such as I still kept in garrison.

This interval continued so long (I mean between Sir Humphrey Gilbert's going from me, and Sir John Perrot's[66] coming to me, who was sent to be Lord President in Munster, a very little before my departure out of Ireland; this valiant and politique knight so persecuted the traitor as in short time, though not in my time, he brought him to come on his knees unto him, and to make a very lowly submission, with very vile conditions for him; under which the rebel lived a small time there, and ran away with wife and children, first into Brittany, then into Portugal, lastly into Rome, and got to him the association of that good man Thomas Stukely;[67] and what he did further in foreign parts, or practised in Ireland, I will not write of, for that I was then out of office, and you know (Sir) better than I. But for Sir John Perrot, I assure you he did most notable, as well in martial actions as politique constitutions, and, in my opinion, he is the most complete and best humoured man to deal with that nation that I know living.

Then departed I from Limerick to Dublin, and there arrived; where I had made but a short abode, but I was advertised of the Earl of Thomond's revolt and adherence to James FitzMaurice; alleging the cause of his rebellion to be the hard dealing of Sir Edward Fitton, then lord president in Connaght and Thomond, where indeed he ministered nothing but justice, and that too mildly. But in truth, the earl violently resisted the president and crossed him.

I finding that besides him I had irons enough in the fire, practised by all peaceable means that I could to appease him, and for the better doing of the same I went to the Queen's house of Laghlyn [*Leighlen*] Bridge, having with me divers of her majesty's council, where I sent for the Earl of Ormond to come to me; and, after consultation had with him, I sent him, joining with him Mr Rauf Rugby [*Rokeby*],[68] then chief justice in Connaght, in commission to parley with Thomond, whom they found to stand upon very obstinate and arrogant terms, avowing that he would never live under a president, nor suffer sessions, writ nor law to be ministered in his country but by himself; for which, being sharply rebuked by the Earl of Ormond, he answered boldly, affirming that he had done nothing but by the Earl of Ormond's counsel. There were present when he so spoke, besides the earl, Mr Rugby, Patrick Sherlock[69] and Oliver Grace; Mr Rugby understood no Irish—the other two were that countrymen born; the words were spoken in Irish, which the Earl of Ormond interpreted into English, and in great haste told him he lied, and called him as he was, traitor; and so brake off that colloquy.

Then was I forced to make head against Thomond, and whereas before I was wont to send into Connaght, justices, lawyers, clerks and pen-men, I was now fain to send horsemen and footmen, munition and shot, pikes, &c., and so grew it to a good sharp bickering, sufficient to be called a battle. Sir Edward Fitton was at it; I could not be there in person, for that I had not yet gotten sufficient handfast of the Butlers. It was well fought on both sides, the Irish giving the charge, but so prevailed the valour of the soldiers, and some loyal men of Connaght, as they brake the Irishry both horsemen and galloglas, and had the killing of as many of them as saved not their lives by running away.

Captain Collier, [Callough] McTurlough, captain of my galloglas, Thomas Le Strange, sometime and many years my household servant, and Patrick Cusake, a good gentleman of the English Pale, did that day very valiantly. Captain Collier was hurt in the body with a bullet; Mr Strange in the face with a Scottish arrow, and the other two slain, and some other tall soldiers of our side. This was fought at a place called the Shroure [Shrule Castle, County Galway], in the confines of Clan-rickarde and MacWilliam Eighter's country [*Iochtar*: Lower: see note

Narrative

93 below]; whither came to the aid of Thomond a great many Scots, who did most of the hurt that was done to the Englishmen, which they dearly paid for that day.

I ceased not to firk [drive, beat] Thomond in his own country, by two of his own kinsmen, the one being his uncle, the other his cousin germain, as well born in blood as he, but my faithful and true servants, called Teg mack Morogh O'Breene and Teg mack Conogher O'Breene; they so applied him that they forced the lubber to leave the land and creep into a French bark that lay in the river of Shannon, and so went into France.[70]

I thus lying in Dublin, long looked for the coming of the Butlers, who at the last came, Sir Edmund and Piers, but my pretty and foregrown page would never come at me, notwithstanding the earl his brother's bond. I had the two brothers indicted of high treason, which they humbly and publicly confessed at the bar. Then, waiving the great mercy of the Queen's Majesty before mentioned, and her highness's direction expressed by letters, I stayed any further proceeding with them by ordinary course of law, but detained them in prison. Shortly after this the Earl of Ormond, according to her majesty's large licence that he might return into England, without further leave or passport obtained of me, went thither, pretending his going was to obtain pardon for his brothers.

Then I summoned according to the laws of that realm, and authority granted by letters patent, a parliament. And, before the first day of the session of the same, I went northward to Armagh, and there had meeting with Turlo Lenogh, who then brought his wife [Agnes Campbell] with him, before mentioned, to be in Scotland at the time of my arrival. Truly (Sir) I found her a good counsellor to him, a well-wisher to peace, and a reverent speaker of the Queen's majesty. She would still persuade him to content himself to be a subject, and to contain him in all his actions like a loyal subject; alleging many examples of her own country of Scotland, where there was many as great potentates as he was, and her own brother or nephew, the Earl of Argyle (I wot not whether), but daughter she was to an Earl of Argyle, who challenged as much *jura regalia*,[71] and other sovereignties, as he could, and yet contented themselves to submit their causes to the laws of the realm, and themselves to the king's pleasure. In truth (Sir) she was a grave, wise and well-spoken lady, both in Scots-English and French, and very well mannered. To be short with him, I concluded even as I desired, which conclusion was in good form written, and I think yet remains extant.

I then returning to Dublin, went southward, peaceably keeping sessions in the counties of Kildare, King's County, and Queen's County; still having with me that good and best approved counsellor that ever was of that country birth, Sir Lucas Dillon; and in all those counties took orders between party and party, as quietly as presently I can do in Wales. I went into Upper Ossory, where I found the noble baron thereof, that true, civil and loyal subject, Sir Barnaby FitzPatrick, most ready to do any service that I could command him. Thither came to me O'Carroll and Mackoglan [*MacCoghlan*], and all three of them waited on me to the good town of Kilkenny, where I remained I suppose between fifteen and twenty days, holding in that time a royal session, in which were indicted, arraigned, condemned and executed above sixty persons, and many of them the stoutest of the Butlers' galloglas, and few of them but for their rebellion; besides a great many hanged by martial law. The session finished I came to Laghlyn [*Leighlin*] Bridge, where I had before me the principal gentlemen of the county of Washford [*Wexford*], and the chieftains of the three septs or lineages of the Cavanaghes, the O'Moroghes and the Kenshelaghes; and for all matters as well to keep peace as resist war, I took such orders as I listed, and they allowed them and obeyed. There (with some cunning) I got to come to me (without protection or other assurance) two brothers, dangerous men, called Kaer [*Cahir*] mac Kedo O'Moore, and Lysagh mac Kedo O'Moore, sons of Kedo, sometime captain of Leysh, and died in rebellion.[72] Lysagh I had tried in Carlogh [*Carlow*] for offences done in that county, and there hanged. Kaer I carried with me to Dublin, where he was tried upon an indictment of treason, and then hanged, drawn and quartered. In this journey I did as good service as ever I did in any peaceable progress.

Thus lying at Dublin, Sir Edmund Butler, being prisoner in the castle, hearing that the earl his brother was gone into England, having too much liberty, wearing no irons, nor locked up in any chamber, but had leave to use the walk on the wall, only guarded with two of my men, whom I thought to have been more vigilant than I found them; practised, by a little boy whom they allowed him, to have a small cord, I am sure not so big as my little finger; found a time when I was returned from taking pleasure abroad in the fields in an evening about Allhallowtide; slipped by the same cord over the castle wall of Dublin, a wall I am sure as high or higher than any about the Tower of London; yet ere he came to the ground by three fathom, the cord broke, and he with the fall sore bruised, leaving behind one of his mittens which he had prepared to slip down the cord, and much blood.

Hot sute [*pursuit*] was made after him, and, as he himself confessed, he heard the trampling of their horses, and their speeches, whom I sent to recover him if they could; but he went on in the dark of the night till he came to the bridge of the water of Dodder, a mile and a half distant from the castle of Dublin, and there, what mad toy soever took him in the head I cannot tell, he went into the river, and there stood (as he constantly after affirmed) the most part of that cold and long night in the water up to the chin. From thence he crept away, and by the help of Hugh MacShane's children[73] he was conducted into the county of Kilkenny, and in the confines of the same was secured and closely kept. For, though I did the best I could, I never could get him during that my deputation. By this may appear the guiltiness of his conscience, and my measuring of justice to him and his brother Piers, for before his escape I had enlarged Piers. But, good Sir, what case had I been in, if he had broken his neck or otherwise killed himself in that mad and desperate adventure? I think I should hardly have made my very friends to have believed otherwise than that I had done it, or caused it to be done, and that the cord hung there but for a colour. He has since told me, and said it likewise to others, that it was written to him often out of England, and told him in the castle, that undoubtedly I would kill him.

Now approached the parliament, in which what acts were made may appear and be extant in the printed book of statutes. Of which printing I was the first author, I am sure to the benefit of the subjects of that land.[74] In which parliament were acts made I know to the advantage of the crown, country and people, invented and set down by myself; namely the attainder of that arch-rebel, Shane O'Neill, giving to her highness and her successors for ever, all his lands and seigniories in fee simple, Clandeboy, &c. Also the lands of the late rebels the Butlers, and Quemberford's [*Comerford's*] lands, and I suppose others of the county of Kilkenny, and others as I think in that county or the county of Tipperary. Likewise was given in that parliament to her majesty and successors the lands of the White Knight and the Knight of the Valley, and they attainted with others as far as I remember. Hereby (as I take it) Her Majesty won both honour, land and revenue; for greedily were those lands sought for all the while I was there; and what hope the Earl of Essex had, taking but a small part of the same so given her by that parliament, his enterprise and proceedings manifested. And surely feasible it was to have done good of it, with lesser charge than he spent about [it].

In the same parliament there was an act made that no linen or woollen yarn should be transported out of that realm unwrought; which, I am sure, would have been the beneficialest act for that country that ever was made, for the suppression of idleness and profit of the people, with gain by custom to the Queen.[75] For while it stood uninterrupted (which was but a few months) there were set up above 100 looms of the one kind and the other, and the cloth made there sold at Bristol and other places. I caused to plant and inhabit there about forty families of the reformed churches of the Low Countries, flying thence for religion sake, in one ruinous town called Swords: and truly (Sir) it would have done any man good to have seen how diligently they wrought, how they re-edified the quite spoiled old castle of the same town, and repaired almost all the same, and how godly and cleanly they, their wives and children lived. They made diapers [tablecloths] and ticks for beds [bedsheets], and other good stuff for man's use; as excellent good leather of deer skins, goat and sheep fells, as is made in Southwark.

This good act did Sir William Gerrard,[76] then lord chancellor of Ireland, utterly overthrow by obtaining a licence of Her Majesty to transport a number of packs of yarn unwrought; for I had by the same act restrained myself and successors for ever to grant any like licence, leaving it always in the power of the Sovereign, as reason was, to do their pleasures. The licence was counted worth five thousand marks, what he made of it I cannot tell; sued for it was without my privity, and granted without my counsel.

One other act I devised, which was the imposition of a custom to be paid for wines, to be discharged within that realm;[77] the limiting but sixteen cities and towns in the same realm to have ships with wines unladen in, as by the act in the printed book may appear, I being the first that caused the laws of that realm to be put in print. This custom is the readiest revenue that Her Majesty has in all Ireland, and for so much the best of any one nature of rents casual: for I am credibly advertised that since the making of that statute, yearly has been answered to Her Majesty's Treasurer £2,000 sterling. And I upon my credit affirm unto you that I might have £2,000 in ready gold to have been silent in the cause, not to have stayed the giving of the royal assent to it, when it had passed by voice of the two houses, but only that I would not have husbanded the cause by the means I could with the principal in credit of either house.

During this session and about the beginning of the same, came to me the Earl of Clancare, from the uttermost part of Munster to Dublin, and there most humbly confessed his rebellion, alleging that Sir Edmund Butler was the cause thereof, in that he reported to him those foolish and frivolous speeches of [concerning] the Earl of Leicester and me, as is before mentioned, and with tears seemed to be sorry for the same; and in most lowly manner that might be devised, he submitted himself, goods, lands and life to Her Majesty, protesting he was not worthy to enjoy any of them, but had most shamefully forfeited them all, in that he had offended Her Majesty in so high a degree of treason, at whose hands he had received such degree and nobilitation. And when he had uttered his mind on this manner in English in far other and better terms than I thought he could, for that he saw many in the chamber in Irish mantles, whereof indeed there were some of right good account, he desired that he might reiterate there his former speeches in the Irish tongue, which he did with so good words and gesture as they that understood him and were of judgement wondered at it. And being bid by me to stand (he still kneeling all this while), he said he would not, nor was not worthy to kneel upon any ground of Her Majesty's, but rather to make his submission lying prostrate in the vilest dunghill in his own country, and besought me that he might do the like which he had done there (being the chamber of the Queen's presence) in the Cathedral Church of that city, which the morrow afterwards he did in form or better than he had done before, in the presence of the best then thereabouts, and of a multitude of others. This act I left registered, and I think remains of record.

Towards the end of this parliament came the ox, I should say Earl, of Thomond, having found that he could find nothing in France, but according to his worth suffered to live there without relief. He made such mien to the then lord ambassador in France [Sir Henry Norris] as he obtained of her Majesty over-great grace, and most gracious letters to me, with some reference to use my discretion; which my discretion was that he should, as well in the chamber of her presence in the castle of Dublin as in the high Church of Dublin, called Christ Church, submit himself as a rebel and traitor and resign into her highness's hands all his lands, castles and seigniories, which he did, and as it seemed penitently. As I had him before in prison, so I kept him still, and his castles warded by my men, whom he victualled, namely Bunratty, Clare and Clonrawd.[78] This as the other I caused, and I think so remains recorded.

Well, Sir, by this you may perceive that during and among my almost continual martial garboils [tumults] I was not altogether sluggish in politique and profitable business, and brought them to some perfect and established end. But notwithstanding all this, the Earl of Ormond (my professed foe) sometime with clamour, but oftener with whispering, did bitterly backbite me; saying that his brethren were driven by my cruelty to rebel, and that he nor his could never have any justice of me, nor any constituted by me in authority to minister justice. And according to his piquant speeches I had sour letters, which in truth to me were tortuous, for (*oi me!*) [*term of exasperation, Greek in origin*] when my designs were reasonable, my proceedings painful, and my success and the event both profitable and honourable, what should I or can I say more but *miserere nobis Domine* [pity us, O Lord]. Thus tired with toil of mind and body in that cursed country, I once again procured and obtained my revocation from the same, and came to the court; where, after more cold acceptation than I hoped for, it was of some often and in many places said, as I before recited, that the Butlers' war was made by my malice borne to them, and that else there was little or nothing done. *Melius merui* [I deserved better].

Now (Sir), I know not by what destiny, but ill enough I am sure for me, nor how things went and were governed when I was from thence, but I was not at home many months unsent for, for consultation sake for the affairs of that country, and caused to attend at the court, and in that sort oftentimes to my great charge, without any allowance; for there was some in great authority that had no will that I should go thither; and so upon every letter of *omnia bene*, I was dismissed without reward; and, being thus wearied with often sending for to no purpose, I resolved to go thither again; the place, I protest, before God, which I cursed, hated and detested, and yet confess with supposition that I could do that which had not been done before, and in great hope hit where others had missed; and so eftsoons the third time I took upon me that thankless charge, and so taking my leave of Her Majesty, kissing her sacred hands with most gracious and comfortable words, departed from her at Dudley castle, passed the seas, and arrived the thirteenth of September 1575, as near the city of Dublin as I could safely; for at that time the city was grievously infected, and so was the English Pale round about the same on every side, with the contagion of the pestilence, whereof there died many daily.

I went to Tredath [*Drogheda*] and, as soon as I could, received the sword of the then Deputy, and taking some order for the peaceable and politique government of the English Pale, and after conference had with the Earl of Essex, for the best possession I could put him in of his country of Farney, parcel of the attainted lands late remembered and given him by Her Majesty, I journeyed to Carregfergus with a competent company of the garrison, all sorts of warlike men as well landlords as followers of that tract attending upon me; from where (after a few days sojournance) I went through Clandeboy, the Glens, and into the Route. There had I interparlance by commissioners with the Scot Sorley Boy,[79] then grown a strong man proud and stubborn; for, not two days after my arrival, and before I had received the sword, he had defeated a company of footmen left there as parcel of the Earl of Essex's regiment, led by Captain John Norreys,[80] but he was not at the defeat, but in the English Pale; his men were commanded by a lieutenant of his, a certain Italian, who, his company said, ran full foully away.

And for that I was not in very good case to make war with the Scot at that time, and finding him desirous of peace, and largely offering to hold the Glens and Route of the queen by rent and service; and for that I was not well assured of Turlo Lenough, who was then also grown proud and strong; I was content for the time to temporise with the Scot, and made as sure covenants as I could with him for observation of the peace, which in truth he observed as long as I was there, suffering anything that was bred or made under his rule to come and be sold at Carregfergus (God knows at easy prices), and would buy such things as he needed in the same town, and pay truly for it.

He humbly and very earnestly desired to have again the island of Raghlyns [*Rathlin*] which his ancestors had occupied seven or eight score years before, and claims it as their rightful inheritance; wherein the Earl of Essex had in the time of his general enterprise for Ulster planted a garrison,* and indeed to good purpose, that enterprise proceeding, but it ceasing, to none at all but a great charge, needless and

---

* Marginal note: 'This appears by a letter of Walter, Earl of Essex to Q. Elizabeth, ult. July 1575.'

lost: and therefore I removed the soldiers and returned to Carregfergus; where, after I had taken order as well with the garrison as the country, the one very willing to serve the other with all kind of victual at very low prices, and the other very willing to defend the countrymen and keep good order among them; in very good order I left the town. And then intending to go to Dublin, where by that time the plague was somewhat ceased; but by the time I came to the Newry (Sir Nicholas Bagenal's house) Turlo Lenough sent a very trusty agent of his to me, with letters of great credence, desiring me that I would come to Armagh where he and his wife would not fail to meet.

Albeit I much disdained to turn my foot backward, and having a great mind southward, for that I heard the Earl of Desmond was grown somewhat insolent and like enough to play such parts as since he did, I thought good to grant Turlo's request, and went to Armagh, where he and the lady his wife gave me reverent meeting, ratifying the former peace made by me in the other time of my government, saving for the service of MacGuire, which, as it appeared, the Earl of Essex in the time of his generalship had given him. He desired to be nobilitated by the title of an earl, and to hold his lands of the Queen by rent and service.[81] The Scots sent their agents to me, craving that they might enjoy the land they occupied, and to yield rent and service for it. And the lady, Turlo's wife, as earnestly suing that she might have the same lands assured to her children, which she had by James MacConnell [MacDonald],[82] Sorley's eldest brother, and I would give more for it than he would. The MacQuillans of the Route came also to me, whom I settled in their country.

Thus leaving all things in the north in good quiet, and yet left such a pick between Turlo and Sorley as within one month after, Turlo (with the aid of some Englishmen whom I suffered him to hire) killed a great number of the best of Sorley's men, and his best and eldest son, to the great weakening of the Scots. I journeyed towards Dublin, doing justice in the counties of Louth and Meath. From Dublin I wrote of my proceeding with Turlo and the Scots; for Turlo he was thought too base to receive such nobilitation; for the Scots it was deemed too dangerous a course to grant them plantation in Ireland; but yet I thank God I satisfied them, and kept that country in quiet as long as I tarried there.

And now albeit it was in the deep of winter, I travelled towards Cork, keeping sessions in the counties of Kildare, Carlow, King's County and Queen's County; and took order with the Baron of Upper Ossory, O'Carroll, MacCoghlan, O'Molloy, Macgoghigan [*MacGeoghegan*] and Shenogh, in English called the Fox.[83] With O'Magher and O'Dwyer I might not deal, for that they were of the county palatine of the Earl of Ormond, in truth the very gall or rather poison of all Munster.

From thence I went to Waterford and sojourned there some days. Hither came to me the Lord Poer and Sir James FitzGarrett [FitzGerald], then lord of the Decies, his brother the Viscount of the same being dead. The Lord Power convited [invited] me to his house, and there made me great and civil cheer. These two noblemen with many other principal gentlemen of that county attended upon me from Waterford through that county, where I had constituted an Englishman to be sheriff, who had his tourns [legal circuits] and courts as well kept and observed or better than in the English Pale.

I went to Dungarvan, where then ruled the renowned soldier, Harry Davells,[84] so exceedingly well as he is worthy immortal good report. There I lay some nights and took order for the fortifying of the town and repairing the castles, as well by heightening the walls and flanking the same and strengthening their gates. Somewhat I gave them, but for every penny that I gave them they spent a shilling, which hath done good since as well appears, for it has held itself unhurted, whereas, since my coming away, Yoghill, being a far stronger town than it was, and more populous, has been twice burned and spoiled. Whither from thence I went, being at that time a good and a rich town, and so to Lismore, and Lisfinnen, where at that time dwelt Sir John of Desmond, then in all appearance a good and a loyal subject, who with the gentlemen and horsemen from that part of the county of Cork, attended me from his house, where he made me exceeding good cheer, until I came to the city of Cork, I think three or four days from Christmas, and there lay till it was Candlemas.

By the way I should tell you how I was entertained at the Viscount Barry's[85] house, called Barry's Court, where I lay three or four nights so exceedingly well as it passed expectation; the people of the city said there never was such a Christmas kept in the same; for there was with me the Earl of Desmond, the Earl of Clancare, the Viscount Barry, the Viscount Roche, Macarthy Reagh, Sir Cormock MacTege [MacCarthy], then Sheriff of the county of Cork, and then and yet Lord of Muskery; the Lord Baron FitzMaurice of Kerry; the Lord Courcy; Condon, but truly written Canton,[86] a great landlord in that country; and all their ladies and wives, and all the captains and principal gentlemen of the MackSwynes, captains of galloglas, who are a strong lineage, and counted manful men in the country; with the rest of the petty lords before written of in the time of my first deputation. Finally there came to me such a number of noblemen, principal gentlemen, horsemen and galloglas as the city could not hold them, so as I might have thought myself rather in the city and county of York, than in the city and county of Cork. I found such humbleness in them and willingness to become English, and accordingly to live under English law, and by the same to be defended, each weaker from his stronger neighbour, as I did ask nothing but it was granted; insomuch as they yielded to bear soldiers as well lying in their own country, as to deliver food for horse and man, being placed elsewhere out of their own countries; which they bare and obeyed while I was there, and I do not fear but they do so still, saving such as have burst into actual rebellion.

During my abode in that city, I heard that the Seneschal of Imokilly,[87] a Garrandyne [*Geraldine*] by race, of the surname of Clangibbon, a capital rebel, had bravely boasted that he would keep his strong castle of Ballymartyr against me; and accordingly had well stuffed and furnished it with bases and small shot, men, munition and victual. I thought not good to leave it unattempted, nor attempting it unwon, and for that I would work the surer; besides my field pieces before mentioned, I carried thither by sea a good fair culverin [a heavy cannon], with powder and bullet good store; and there came with me of the townsmen of Cork 150 or 200 well appointed and arrayed men.

I approached the castle, being very high and strong, and planted my artillery as near as I could, and lively my men went to work, which cost some good ones of them their lives, for the rebels shot freshly out of the castle both bases and small shot, where the stout and fast cannoner, old Thomas Eliott, now a suitor at the court, was stricken through the thigh. The culverin made such bouncing at the walls, the saker and minions such rattling at the roof and casework, as the rebels were so afraid that in the night, my watch being negligent, they stole away, leaving the house, as afore is written, well victualled. There I left a ward, which continued long after, and went back again to Cork.

From thence I went to the Viscount Roche's,[88] and there was passingly entertained; and from thence to the town of Kilmallock, being in the county of Limerick, all the way being attended upon by the most or at last by the principal and best of the forenamed personages. I remained in Kilmallock two or three days, and thither came to me all the best and principallest gentlemen of that side of the county of Limerick, who attended me unto the same city; there I remained I think a week, found great obedience and willingness to do anything that I would have done; they submitted themselves to any taxation for bearing of soldiers that I would impose upon them.

Thither came to me all the chiefest gentlemen of the other side of that county, and of Kerry and Conylough [*Conello*], and the freeholders of the Knight of the Valley's country, the name of which I do not now remember.[89] Likewise there came three or four bishops of the provinces of Cashel and Tuam which bishops (albeit they were Papists) submitted themselves unto the queen's majesty, and unto me her deputy, acknowledging that they held all their temporal patrimony of the queen's majesty, and desired humbly that they might (by her highness) be inducted into their ecclesiastical prelacy. Here was some hold between the bishops and me, too long to be recited; for they stood still upon *Salvo suo ordine, &c.*, and I of the queen's absolute authority.[90]

I at that time took order for the re-edifying of the long-ruined castle of the same city, which (before I left the land) was in effect finished; what hath been done on it since, I wot not. This done, I went into

Thomond, where the earl met me, albeit he had come to me unto the city of Limerick before, and reverently and in good sort used and entertained me, for as before is written, I had counterpoised his force with his own kinsfolk's before armed. I there subdued a rebellious race of the surname of the earl, the O'Briens; their captains were called the bishop's sons,[91] and indeed the bastards they were of a bishop of Killaloe, which bishop was son to an O'Brien, captain of Thomond. Of this wicked generation some I killed, some I hanged by order of law, but all I subdued; and so leaving that country in quiet, which is a great one, and by me made a county of the name of the county of Clare, I went out of the same into O'Siagnes' [*O'Shaughnessy's*] country,[92] which I found all in garboil and violent wars. The captain whereof (as I thought he ought to be, his brother being dead, and having before served my Lord of Leicester) I settled in his due room, and quieted all the rest; and so went to the good town of Galway; in the way to which met me the Earl of Clarickard, mine old acquaintance, in very reverent manner, and attended me to Galloway, where I remained I wot not how many days, but with most humble submission; namely, MackWilliam Eughter of English race,[93] and by surname Borough, there called Burke, but in Latin anciently and modernly written De Burgo; and with him a number of petty landlords of sundry surnames, the most English, and many of his own surname. There came to me also Mack-eorish, of English surname Brymicham [*Bermingham*]; Mac-Jordan, of English surname De Exeter; Mackostilogh, of English surname De Angulo or Nangle; Mackeviley, of English surname Staunton; MackMorris of English surname, Prendergast, and should before have remembered MackPhilippin, by English surname a Burke, and of English race. All these submitted and seemed desirous to live in loyalty, and under the laws and subjection of the crown of England, detesting and abhorring their degeneration and inveterate barbarity.

The Earl of Clanrickard, as he said, caused his two most bad and rebellious sons, Ulick and John,[94] to come to me, with humble submission; whom I would to God I had then hanged, but their submission (with over-much clemency) I accepted. Albeit I committed them, and in the chief church of the town had a sermon made of them and their wickedness, by a countryman of their own called Lynch,[95] sometime a friar in Greenwich, but a reformed man, a good divine and preacher in the three tongues, Irish, English and Latin. The young men publicly in the church I rebuked very sharply, and they as humbly submitted, and again to prison I committed them. And having settled every thing in Galway, in effect as I would have it, I departed from thence, dismissing Mac-William Euter and the forenamed sober barons.

I should have remembered that [Sir Hugh] O'Donnell came thither to me, with great show of courtesy and kindness to me, and likewise [Sir Donough] O'Connor Sligo, who faithfully promised their perseverance in loyalty, which they have for ought that I know ever since performed. And so travelling toward A[th]lone, I was convited by the Earl of Clanrickard to his house of Balie Logh Reogh [*Loughrea*], still leading with me his two sons as prisoners in my marshal's ward. In his house he did most honourably entertain me, and attended upon me till I came to A[th]lone, where I used him as familiarly and friendly as I could, telling him with as good and loving speech as I was able to utter (for of very old acquaintance we were), what love I bore him, and that if he would take upon him the government of Connacht, and suppress the most vile and tyrannical extortion of coyne and livery, I would make him governor under the deputy of that province. He coldly thanked me; accept it he would not, his reasons for which are not worth the writing. His sons I still led with me, captives upon their oath and his promise that they should never pass the river of Shannon, nor come into Connacht without my special licence in writing; and thus in friendly manner we departed, I to Dublin with his two sons prisoners, and he home with his friends and followers, where I used John at my table friendly, and Ulick as my well-looked-on servant, and at last licensed them to live with their friends, so as they exceeded not their forenamed and appointed bounds.

I had not been long at Dublin but I heard of some disorders of the Cavanaghs and some of the good county of Washford [*Wexford*], unto which I addressed myself, and having gone one day's journey southward towards them, I was credibly advertised of the revolt of the two young Clanrickardines before named, albeit they were mortal enemies, though brethren, yet *in odium tertie nempe*[96] the Queen and English government, they connived and joined in actual rebellion; shaking off and cutting in pieces their English garments upon the river of Shannon, saying that those should be their pledge for their remaining by east Shannon.

The first memorable act that they, or one of them at least, did, which I am sure was John, was that they or he went to Balieanrhie [*Athenry*], a very ancient English town, in English 'the king's town', a great town, and by their English ancestors founded, amplified, and with bloody battles defended against the Irishry. In this town was the sepulchre of their forefathers, and the natural mother of the same John buried; the chief church of which town they most violently burned; and being told and besought that he would spare the burning of the church where his mother's bones lay, he blasphemously swore, that if she were alive and in it, he would burn both the church and her too, rather than any English churl should inhabit or fortify there. I had there some workmen, whom they most cruelly killed; and indeed I had begun some fortifications there, but finish it I did not; worthy the finishing it is, if the reformation of Ireland be worth the consideration.

Thus advertised I diverted my course from the south into the west, and that with such expedition as I was there before they looked for me, and brake off some of their intended enterprise. I passed the river of Shannon, I went to the Earl of Clanrickard's chief house beforenamed, I broke it, and took him, he protesting ignorance and innocence, but God knows untruly, and so has since most manifestly been proved. I proclaimed the sons rebels and traitors, and committed, led away and still detained the father; I planted there two worthy and sufficient gentlemen, namely Thomas Le Strange and Captain Collier, with a garrison of 250 men, who valiantly did their devoir as well in offending the rebels as in defending the subjects. I sent for the earl's followers to come to Galway, as well English as Irish, whose names I have forgotten, saving one Mackuge [*MacHugh*] and Mackremmon [*MacRedmond*].[97]

There came to me also a most famous feminine sea captain, called Grany I'Malley [Grace O'Malley],[98] and offered her services unto me, wheresoever I would command her, with three galleys and two hundred fighting men, either in Ireland or Scotland. She brought with her her husband, for she was as well by sea as by land more than master's mate with him. He was of the nether Burkes, and now as I hear MackWilliam Euter, and called by nickname Richard in Iron.[99] This was a notorious woman in all the coast of Ireland: this woman did Sir Philip Sydney see and speak with; he can more at large inform you of her.

Here heard we first of the extreme and hopeless sickness of the Earl of Essex, by whom Sir Philip being often most lovingly and earnestly wished and written for, he with all the speed he could make went to him, but found him dead before his coming, in the castle at Dublin.

From thence I marched with horsemen and footmen in prosecution of the rebels, but overtake them I could not; divers castles I won from their party takers [supporters], and with a long and painful journey at the last I came to a strong castle called Castle Barry, the which I besieged, for held it was and wrongfully from MackWilliam Euter, then being in the camp with me. In the night the rebels set the castle on fire and stole away in the smoke; the castle I delivered to MackWilliam Euter.[100] And divers others of either race aforesaid would not come at me; to those that came I manifested the rebellion of the sons of their landlord, and detected his disloyalty as well as I could, specially being descended of so noble an English surname as he and some of them were; they seemed all to be sorry for it, and promised and swore loyalty, and some of them performed it.

And so departing, leading the earl with me, leaving the town and castle of Balie Logh Reagh well stuffed with men and munition, and fortified more than needed against any Irishmen, and victualled so far above ordinary for the owner, as it might well appear that it was for an extraordinary and unlawful extent; I took, before I went, his castles of Clare and Balieslough [*Ballinasloe*], the one being within six miles of Galway, the other within twelve miles of A[th]lone, the uttermost confines of his country. I garrisoned them with soldiers, and left them furnished, and at the commandment of the two gentlemen before named. These gentlemen did sundry notable exploits against the rebels worthy commendation and memory.

I caused a bridge to be begun at that time over the great river of Sowke [*Suck*], hard by the castle of Balislogh, which since was perfected by the worthy soldier, counsellor, and colonel, Sir Nicholas Malby, who finished my work, and a good work, for after I had settled him in that province, I had no cause to care for that province, as it well proved by the valiant overthrows of the rebels, politique pacification, large and great inhabitations, rents and services revived, and newly erected and still continued, out of which he receives his entertainment to his contentation, which never was before my government; and thus I left that province of Connaght. To make short, having been too tedious with you, under the government of this good knight Sir Nicholas Malby, who if he had continued longer in the charge of Munster, the crown of England had not spent so much, nor the good subjects of Ireland suffered so much, as since the withdrawing him from that place they have; you know this, Sir, peradventure better than I.

And being in the city of Dublin, I grew weary of idleness; for albeit the wars were somewhat hot in Connaght, yet was the diligence and activity such of Sir Nicholas Malby, as neither the English Pale or army felt it, other than such as were of his own particular regiment, for he so well governed the good subjects as they were contented to yield unto him service, victual and wages, and those my impositions I think holden yet: and the rebels and their favourers be so persecuted as he fed most upon them and made gain of them.

I leaving the city of Dublin, journeyed in peaceable manner through the counties of Kildare, Carlogh, Kilkenny and Washford, in all places holding sessions by commission of *oyer* and *terminer*[101] as orderly and civilly as it had been in England, and had great and civil appearance of gentlemen and freeholders, who yielded very just trial of malefactors.

I came home by the sea side, through the countrey called Base Leinster, in a general word, but particularly the Kavenaghes, then ruled by Captain Thomas Masterson[102] and well were they ruled, for the people were obedient, quiet and rich. Then through the O'Moraghes' [*MacMurroughs'*] country, governed by Richard Synod,[103] a gentleman of the county Washford. I went through the three countries of the Kynchiloghes [*Kinsellas*], where Thomas Masterson was captain, and so into the O'Byrnes' country, and through the O'Tooles' country, then governed by the good captain and counsellor, Francis Agard,[104] and so home to Dublin.

In truth, Sir, all these Irish people, albeit their country were not shired, yet lived they as loyally as any people in the shire ground, and they entertained me as well (when I travelled among them) as I could wish to be entertained anywhere. They were rich, and everything plentiful in their country, no waste land but (as they term it there) it bare corn or horn. And whereas they were wont to buy their bread in Dublin, or barter for the same by giving fire-wood, they were then able to sell corn not only in Dublin, but by boats to send it to Carrigfergus and other parts of the north of Ireland where corn was dear.

Being thus in great quiet in the English Pale, and all the same in such wealth and quiet manurance of their soil as the oldest man alive never saw it in the like, some of the barons and other principal gentlemen thereof grudged greatly at the bearing of the soldiers, and made divers grievous complaints in the name of the commons; but indeed the cause was for that the country being reduced into such quiet as they mistrusted no wars to come, loathed then those who had brought them to the same, which was the army, and looked to exact all that of the poor commons which they yielded to the finding of the soldiers.

When they found that their complaints prevailed not, they fell to exclamation, and manifestly to impugn the Queen's prerogative, saying that the Queen had no such by law as to impose any charge upon the subject, without consent of parliament. I had in this few helpers, for truly there was few in the English Pale thoroughly sound for the Queen's prerogative and profit, saving Sir Lucas Dillon and his whole lineage, far the best of that country breed; he and they most manfully and constantly stood with the Queen in defence thereof. The chief opposers of them against the Queen were the Baron of Delvin,[105] the cancerdest and most malicious man, both for religion and English government, (I think) that Ireland then bare. There joined with him the Lord of Howth [Thomas St Lawrence], the Lord of Trimbleston [Patrick Barnewall], and the Lord of Killeene [Christopher Plunket] and divers other knights, principal gentlemen and lawyers, among whom Nicholas Nugent, the second baron of the exchequer, and since executed for treason, was one.[106]

Finally, all the principal landlords of the English Pale confederated, and in their conventicles connived against me and her highness's prerogative. There did no nobleman manifest himself to be on the Queen's part, but the Lord of Slane [James Fleming] and the Lord of Upper Ossory [Sir Barnaby FitzPatrick]. Lastly, they concluded and accordingly sent their agents to the Queen's most excellent majesty, exclaiming upon me for my cruel, unlawful and intolerable exactions, with all other defamatory speeches that they could have any colour to speak against me.

Then was I driven to search old records, and so did I many; the which records many years before, I myself being Treasurer there, had laid up, and dressed a house for the conservation of them and others; little thinking then that the Queen's prerogative, of such antiquity as it was proved to be by the same, should ever have been brought in question; but by those ancient records it appeared that imposition there called Cess, from the time of King Edward III at times, and at the appointment of the governor and council, had been used until that time.[107]

In this search the chancellor, then William Gerrard, singularly well did assist me, and in the avouching and pleading the same; and yet afterwards (according to the skittishness of his busy head) he joined with the country, though underhand and secretly, to overthrow my honourable and profitable designs both for the Queen and governor for the time, and for the crown and country for ever, as it manifestly appeared after. I then, to make declaration that I delighted not in the exaction, offered them in sundry public assemblies (that where they had exclaimed that the burden and charge of the Queen's army and my household came to

£10 or £12 sterling upon a plough-land) that I would discharge them for £3 6s 8d sterling the plough-land yearly, to be paid at a day certain.

Yet this contented not the great ones, but still they repined at any charge, terming it to grow upon no just prerogative of the Queen, and to them was an intolerable and endless servitude. But when this matter came into the commons' heads it cannot be told with what joy and plausibility, manifested with letters subscribed with scores and hundreds of names, yea, whole townships, cantreds and baronies, of thanks to me for it. They accepted the same, and readily made payment thereof to the hands of Robert Woodford, an honest and sufficient gentleman yet living, then clerk controller of my household, and appointed collector thereof; who immediately paid it over to Sir Edward Fitton, then Treasurer, as by both their accounts yet extant doth and may appear. When I had brought this to pass I thought I achieved a great enterprise, and accomplished an old conceit of mine own. The sum came to £2,400 sterling, and all paid to the Treasurer saving £100, which was stayed for decision of a controversy about freedom challenged for certain lands, as far as I remember, by the Earl of Kildare and Sir Nicholas Bagenal. The improvement of that rent me thought was honourable and profitable for the Queen, easy for the subject, and good for the governor in respect of having the soldiers in readiness; for the Queen and crown should have had £2,400 sterling more than ever it had, the people should not have paid above twopence sterling out of an English acre, and all this should have lain within six shires of the English Pale.

By this means should the soldiers have been kept together, to the great ease of the country, disburdenment of their boys, whores and dogs, and a number of other insolent actions, which is impossible to bridle them from, unless they lie so together as they may be kept under discipline; service thereby should much have been furthered, for it is better for the governor to serve with 500 so garrisoned and together lodged than with 1,000 over the country dispersed.

But still, and almost weekly, I received to my hearty grief, that I was a costly servant, and alienated from her Highness her good subjects' hearts. Would God the charges of my times were compared with others as well before me as since me, and openly showed, and then I trust I should be more indifferently judged of. And what consolation of these good subjects' hearts has been since my coming away, the quartering and heading of a good many of them has made some show; and more might have been (yea, and justly) if the immense mercy of her majesty had not been. But to whomsoever this device was hard or soft, to use it was most heavy, for I to win this improvement to the Queen and crown for ever, gave over all cess for anything pertaining to my household, but paid ready money for everything, to my undoing.

Now, Sir, to return to the commonwealth-men (for so they called themselves), I mean the messengers of the repining malcontents of the English Pale, who then were at the court, and there had better audience than either they or their cause deserved, and still vexed me with letters carrying matters of hard digestion, and sending copies of the same to their copters [allies], who sometimes published them with triumph over me, upon their ale-benches or elsewhere they would, before I had received the original letter. I thought good partly to justify my doings, but chiefly to maintain Her Majesty's prerogative, and purchase her profit, to send over the lord chancellor with matter of ancient record to reply against the oppositions made by the malcontents against her majesty's prerogative. I furnished him with the aforewritten records, with as good instruction as I could give him, and with honourable allowance by the day as long as he should be employed about that matter, and money out of mine own purse, and sundry bills to be made acts of parliament. Among which one was for the enacting of this new rent or imposition, which I was sure I would have made pass by parliament. He went, and so well did in defence of her highness's right, as two of the three lewd legates,[108] namely, Burnell and Netterville, were committed to the Tower, and the third, the oldest and craftiest of the three, named Barnaby Scurlogh, ordered to submit himself in form, as I would appoint him in Dublin; which he did, and I received in more meek sort than he had deserved of me. For the rest of the chancellor's negotiations I will write nothing, but this, that nothing he did for any other matter according to my instructions, and nothing he brought me back again (not so much as that bill for her Highness's honourable profit), but speeches delivered that it was a thing impossible, a thing intolerable, a matter dangerous, and might breed universal rebellion in the realm. Well he did for himself, for he brought over a licence, which he held at £3,000 to be sold, and was to the utter overthrow of an act made by me in my former government, I am sure the most beneficialest for the commonwealth that ever (any one act) was made. He also brought an order to enlarge, and without my privity in my absence did enlarge, the forenamed repinants, whom I held prisoners in the Castle of Dublin; and to them he would give better countenance than to those who most constantly had stood in defence of the Queen's right, I mean Sir Lucas Dillon and (he that is now) Sir Robert Dillon[109] and the rest of that surname; in truth to the true and sound subjects and advocates, as it well appeared. For as soon as I was gone he made Nicholas Nugent (displaced by me from the second baronship of the exchequer and committed to the Castle of Dublin, where he found him prisoner for his arrogant obstinacy against the Queen) chief justice of the common pleas; and others he placed in good offices whom he knew were neither fast in the Queen's right, nor friendly to me. I wish (sir) I deserved better of William Gerrard than so.

These things I confess had well near broken my heart; and left the sword I would, and gone over without leave, though I had adventured the getting of the Queen's displeasure, and loss of mine own life, had not an obscure and base varlet called Rorie Oge O'Moore[110] stirred. This Rorie was the son of another Rorie, sometime, but never in my time, chief of the O'Moores, and captain of the country called Leish (now the Queen's County), who married the daughter of the Earl of Ormond. This young Rorie, after the execution of his kinsmen before remembered, Caer Mackedo and Lyssa Mackedo, in my absence grew to more strength than was convenient to have been suffered, and called himself O'More, and sought to patronise his worshipful person over and upon the whole country of Lesh. I will not say, though I could probably guess, what counsel he had and assistance to and in that his rebellion; but sure

I am that one Danyell, the Earl of Ormond's secretary, confessed to me, and that *sponte* [of his own accord], the Earl of Ormond had willed and counselled him never to submit himself as long as I or any for me should make war upon him; signifying and prosticating [prophesying] many things, as my disgrace with the Queen, the mislike and likelihood of revolt against me of the English Pale, with many more things too many to be written.

Against this companion I advanced, being of horsemen and footmen a right good force; I went into his fastest places, but never would he fight with me, but always fled, and was secured in the county of Kilkenny, and under and with the Butlers. When I saw that he would not abide me, nor I could not overtake him, and having other matters of great weight for the realm to do, I retired myself and the army, leaving behind me in Mary-Borough, the principal town and fort of that country, my lieutenant Sir Harry Harrington,[111] my most dear sister's son, and likewise lieutenant of the King's County, in old time called Offaly. He so well prosecuted the rebels that in short time he dismounted them all, and drove them to be unarmed and breechless and barefooted footmen, and in very poor and miserable case. But such as my nephew's destiny, and by persuasion of some about him, and his own credulity, that when he had brought the rebel Rorie to so low an ebb, as he besought him to admit him to a conference; after which the traitor said he would submit himself, and the same swore: he came to a parley with him indiscreetly, for there was he taken and carried away captive most vilely, to my heart's grief, for I loved him and do love him as a son of my own; and the rebel kept him most miserable. I wrought and sought his enlargement by the best means I could, but nothing prevailed without such conditions as I would not have enlarged Philip my son.

Then made I as actual and as cunning war as I could upon the vile villainous rebel, and still my men prevailed, but still he kept my nephew miserably, carrying him from place to place most like a slave in deserts vile and most travelsom [troublesome] places; yet through the faithful service of a faithful countryman of mine, a Kentishman, I mean Robert Harpoole,[112] an inveterate soldier of that country, I had harboured this malicious traitor, who had my unfortunate nephew with him. I beset his cabinish dwelling with good soldiers and excellent good executioners; the rebel had within it twenty-six of his best and most assured men, his wife, and his marshal's wife, and Cormagh O'Connor,[113] an ancient and rank rebel, of long maintained in Scotland, and at last (but too soon) reclaimed from thence by the Queen our mistress, and with stipend as a pension sent to Ireland; who, returning to the vomit of his innate rebellious stomach, went to Rorie Oge, and took part with him in his rebellion; and in that place and time was by a man of mine, called John Parker, killed. There was also killed his wife and all his men; only there escaped himself and his marshal, called Shane MacRorye Reogh, in truth miraculously, for they crept between the legs of the soldiers into the fastness of the plashes of trees.

Rorie Oge confessed, and so did the wife of his marshal, whom the soldiers saved, that the skirts of his shirt was with an English sword cut from his bare body; but this assault and conflict being done in the dark night, the villainous rebel fell upon my most dear nephew, being tied in chains and him most shamefully hacked and hewed with my nephew's own sword, to the effusion of such a quantity of blood as were incredible to behold. He brake his arm with the blunt sword, and cut off the little finger of one of his hands, and in sundry parts of his head so wounded him as I myself in his dressing did see his brains moving; yet my good soldiers brought him away, and a great way, upon their halberds and pikes, to a good place in that country, where he was relieved, and afterwards (I thank God) recovered.

During this service, and before his unhappy apprehension, I went to Newry, and thither come to me Turlough Lenogh (the lady his wife not being able to come, through a hurt she had), but well had she counselled him as it appeared, for most frankly and familiarly used he me, coming to me against the will of all his counsellors and followers, protesting he so much trusted and loved me as he would not so much as once ask hostage or protection. He brought above £400 sterling to the town, and spent it all in three days; he celebrated Bacchus's feast most notably and, as he thought, much to his glory; but as many hours as I could get him sober, I would have him into the castle, where he would as reverently (as his little good manners did instruct him) speak of the Queen, craving still and that most humbly, that he might be nobilitated by the Queen, and to hold his lands and seigniories of her majesty by rent and service; and there ratified all former peace made between me and him, and the Earl of Essex and him. Thus he being well satisfied, and I very joyous of so good a conclusion, departed in most loving terms, he to his camp, where among all his people he used a long speech of the majesty of the Queen and my great bounty; indeed some plate and other trifles I gave him. I returned to Dublin, and by the way received letters of my nephew Harrington's unfortunate taking and miserable captivity, which abated great part of my joy. Of his taking, keeping and delivering you have already heard.

Whiles I thus lay at Dublin I understood that the Earl of Desmond still repining at the government of Sir William Drury,[114] and upon a short message sent him by Sir William, fell into a frantic resolution, and whereas he purposed to have kept his Christmas in Youghal, he suddenly brake off that determination and went into Kerry and straightways assembled forces; and had I not taken the ball at the first bound, he had undoubtedly used violence against Sir William Drury and his people, who were not many. I straightways addressed me to Kilkenny, and thither I sent for Sir William Drury, the earl and the countess his wife. They came all to me; the earl was hot, wilful and stubborn; the countess at that time a counsellor. Sir William Drury confessed some fault, but finally (though with much ado) I made them friends, and a sound pacification of all quarrels between them, and sound it continued as long as I continued governor there. But not long after (as you know), upon like occasion as before is noted, he and his two brothers, Sir John and Sir James, fell into actual rebellion, in which the good knight Sir William Drury, then Lord Justice, died; and he, as a malicious and unnatural rebel, still persists and lives.

The Christmas ended, wherein I entertained the earl and the countess as well as I could, and presented them both with silks and jewels, not a little to my costs; I fell then into holding of sessions by commission of *oyer* and *terminer*, but in person I would never be on the bench, for that the Ormonists should not say that I was there by speech or countenance to engrave any matter against them. And though I were as much thwarted by some of them as might be, yet had I a great number of that country indicted, according to the laws arraigned, judged to die and executed, for abetting, favouring and aiding Rorie Oge; this matter remains of record.

Divers of the principal gentlemen would in the night, and as it were disguised, come to me protesting they durst not in the day time be seen to do so, for fear of the Earl of Ormond. They did give me good information of matters of weight, and I them the best instruction I could. The earl in England still exclaimed that I lay there to no other end but to make myself rich by the spoil of his country, saying that I paid for nothing that I took, which was utterly untrue; for not only my household officers but all others that followed me, paid ready money for every thing they took in any town where I came. And when the Earl of Ormond was so said to by Mr Waterhouse,[115] sometime my secretary, he answered that his officers had written so to him: 'Yes, my Lord,' quoth he, 'there is difference between writing unsworn and speaking upon oath, for here is in writing the examination and confession of divers your principal officers, who all not only clear my lord my master and his officers and men of all extortions dealing with any your people or followers, but also affirm that they never wanted justice with favour in all their and your causes.' This (good sir) can Mr Waterhouse declare at large unto you, if it please you to give him the hearing.

After the unfortunate taking of my said nephew Harrington from the rebel, I placed a continual presidie or garrison to persecute the rebel, as with Sir Nicholas Malby, the good Captain Collier, before written of, Captain Furres, the valiant Captain Mackworth and others as I thought good, but lastly and most effectually under the Baron of Upper Ossory, my particular sworn brother, and the faithfullest man for the Queen's service for martial action that ever I found of that country. He so diligently followed and prosecuted the rebel as within a few months with great skill and cunning he harboured him [i.e. ran him to ground], and with as much or more courage assailed him; he not having the third [number of] men the rebel had, as some will say, not the sixth, made the best fight with him that ever I heard of between Irishmen. The slaughter was great on both sides, but the vile rebel Rory was killed by a household servant of the baron's; his marshal aforenamed escaped, and the rebel's body, though dead, so well attended and carried away, as it was the cause of the death of a good many of men on both sides; yet carried away he was. But not long after, his head was sent me and set up upon the Castle of Dublin; for which I had proclaimed 1,000 marks [£666] to be given to him that would bring it to me, and £1,000 to him that would bring him me alive.

The valorous and loyal Baron of Upper Ossory, when I offered him the 1,000 marks (by proclamation promised), answered that he had received by nurture under the good and religious King Edward VIth more good, and by pension greater gain, confirmed by the Queen's most excellent majesty, than his service deserved; and in fine would take but £100 to give among his men which were the fighters; and that I paid him out of mine own purse, and he distributed it to them, most of whom I knew. I could not obtain at any time a letter from her majesty of thanks for this service, nor in long time from the lords of the council. This action thus ended, I loathed to tarry any longer in Ireland, and yet before I went I invaded [Art] MacMahon's[116] country, preyed, burned and totally destroyed the same, in revenge of a shameful murder committed by him in killing a valiant and noble man called the Lord of Louth, and as towardly a young gentleman as ever I knew of the Irishry, son and heir to Sir Hugh MacGennis,[117] knight, lord and captain of the country called Evaugh [*Iveagh*]. I so plagued that vile bloody churl as, within short time after my departing out of Ireland, he came to the Newry to Sir William Drury with a withe [a noose or halter] about his neck, and in that form submitting himself he obtained his pardon, which he knew full well he should never have gotten at my hands, and his withe should ever have served him but only to hang him, for had I tarried but a few months longer, I would have made him answer *secundum jus talionis*.[118]

I loathed, I say again, to tarry any longer in that land, chiefly for that I saw the Queen make so little account of my service in killing that pernicious rebel, and was contented to be persuaded that there was no more difficulty to kill such a rogue as he was than to kill mad George the sweeper of the Queen's court. But such a rogue he was that he burned all the good towns in the counties of Carlow and Kildare, as the town of Carlow and the Naas, &c. He had killed, before I could get himself killed, four hundred fighting men; their names I had in several lists sent me by the several captains aforenamed, and yet all this counted no war, but a chastisement of vagabonds.

It grieved me not a little that Her Majesty rejected those bills which I sent to be allowed to be made laws, whereof many had been devised by me, and by my instruction penned, specially that bill which was to give the Queen the rent before written; which bill I verily think with all the rest were quashed by the advice of that ambitious Chancellor Gerrard. I found so little consideration in the most of the gentlemen of the English Pale, and such unthankfulness in some great ones, both which sorts I had greatly benefited, as I was weary any longer to live among them. It irked me not a little to see the ambitious and disdainful dealings of the chancellor, who glorying of the great credit that he had won of her Majesty (which indeed was more than his worth) that he would not let to say, but not in my hearing, that he had brought over such warrant for himself and restraint for me, as I could do nothing without him; he still hastening me away, gloriously braving behind my back that if I were gone, and the new justice ruling by his direction, Ireland should be governed with a white rod.[119] But the noble knight and warrior Sir William Drury, not many months after my departure, found that he had need to rule with white rods as long as spears and morris-pikes, and with swords whited as white as blood would whiten them; in which service he died, and I would to God the country was yet as well as I left it almost five years ago.

Thus leaving the same in universal quiet, I passed by seas and came into England, carrying with me the old and arch-rebel the Earl of Clanrickard, and a son of his called William, who since for treason and rebellion was a traitor and rebel executed. When I came to the court to know how I was entertained, I confess well, but not so well as I thought and in conscience felt that I had deserved. The arch-rebel whom I brought, the forenamed, you know how and by whom he was countenanced. Lastly, though well approved, and by the most honourable board of the Privy Council, he was enlarged, dismissed and sent home, to my small credit. Notwithstanding all these my painful services, I was accounted *servus inutilis* [prodigal servant], for that I had exceeded a supposed commission; a conference indeed there was that £20,000 should defray all the charges of Ireland, as well ordinary as extraordinary, and of this I oft heard to my great discomfort; the which I answered not either with boast or desert of my service, or showed any great confidence but that it might be, as that it in *prima facie* appeared, that I had exceeded the sum of £20,000 yearly, nor in truth I cared not much, for in sound conscience I felt it, that I had spent nothing but honourably and profitably for the Queen and for the security of the country. And although somewhat I had exceeded in spending Her Majesty's treasure, I had too far exceeded in spoiling my own patrimony; but since being curious to know what the charges were in the time of that my government (by Sir Edward Fitton's accounts, all that time being Treasurer), it appeared that, reasonable and due allowances granted me, I am within the bounds of that £20,000 a year.

This account was there engrossed and sent to my lord treasurer [Lord Burghley], the copy whereof was sent to me by Thomas Jenyson, auditor in Ireland, and his letter written to me with his own hand, purporting the effect of the last-written matter; I have his letter and the copy of the account. But yet I most heartily and lovingly beseech you that you will write to him, willing him to signify unto you truly and at large of the charges of that my time of government; charging him that you have heard that he had written to me in sort as I have declared, which if you shall receive from him in manner as may be to my advantage, I hope you will friendly and brotherly use it to that purpose.

And thus an end of my Irish discourse: and now to my great and high office in Wales which I yet and long have happily and quietly held, having served in it full three and twenty years. A happy place of government it is, for a better people to govern, or better subjects to their Sovereign, Europe holds not. But yet hath not my life been so domestically spent in Wales, and the sweet marches of the same, but that I have been employed in other foreign actions. For besides the three before-mentioned deputations in Ireland, I was twice sent into France; once into Scotland; twice to the seaside to receive the Duke John Casimir and Adolph, Duke of Holst[ein]: these two last journeys, though they were but Kentish, yet were they costly—it may be it was more of a Kentish courage than of deep discretion; well I remember allowance I had none, nor yet thanks. I was sent and did remain a good while at Portsmouth in superintending the victualling of Newhaven. Oftentimes I was sent for and commanded to attend about the court for Irish causes, to my great charges.

Truly (Sir) by all these I neither won nor saved; but now, by your patience, once again to my great and high office; for great it is in that in some sort I govern the third part of this realm under her most excellent majesty: high it is, for by that I have precedence of great personages, and far my betters; happy it is, for the people whom I govern, as before is written; and most happy for the commodity that I have by the authority of that place to do good every day, if I have grace to one or other; wherein I confess I feel no small felicity, but for any profit I gather by it, God and the people (seeing my manner of life) know it is not possible how I should gather any. For alas, Sir, how can I, not having one groat of pension belonging to the office; I have not so much ground as will feed a mutton; I sell no justice; I trust you do not hear of any order taken by me ever reversed, nor my name or doings in any court (as courts there be whereto by appeal I might be called) ever brought in question. And if my mind were so base and corruptible as I would take money of the people whom I command, for my labour (commanded by the Queen) taken among them, yet could they give me none or very little, for the causes that come before me are causes of people mean, base, and many very beggars. Only £20 a week to keep an honourable house, and one hundred marks [£66] a year to bear foreign charges I have; what house I keep I dare stand to the report of any indifferent man, and kept it is as well in mine absence as when I am present, and the councillors fare as well as I can be content to do; but true books of account shall be, when you will, showed unto you, that I spend above £30 a week. Here some may object that I upon the same keep my wife and her followers. True it is, she is now with me, and hath been this half-year, and before not in many years; and if both she and I had our food and house-room free, as we have not, in conscience we have deserved it. For my part I am not idle, but every day I work in my function, and she for her old service and marks (yet remaining in her face) taken in the same merits her meat. When I went to Newhaven I left her a full fair lady, in mine eye at least the fairest, and when I returned I found her as foul a lady as the smallpox could make her; which she did take by continual attendance of her majesty's most precious person (sick of the same disease), the scars of which (to her resolute discomfort) ever since hath done and doth remain in her face, so as she lives solitarily *sicut nicticorax in domicilio suo*,[120] more to my charge than if we had boarded together, as we did before that evil accident happened.

It is now almost one hundred years since this house was erected, and I am well assured that neither the Queen's most honourable household nor any downward to the poorest ploughman's house can be kept as they were forty years ago, yet have I no more allowed me than was allowed forty years ago. I confess I am the meanest and poorest man that ever occupied this my place, and yet I will and may compare I have continued in better and longer housekeeping than any of my predecessors; I have built more and repaired more of her Majesty's castles and houses, without issuing of any money out of her highness's coffers, than all the presidents that have been this hundred years; and this will the view of the castles of Ludlow, the castle of Wigmore and Montgomery, and the house of Tickenhill by Beawdeley [*Bewley*] justify.[121]

And thus I end any further treating of my other great office of Wales, confessing both the one and the other to have been too high and too honourable for so mean a knight as I am; yet how I managed these offices I will take no exception to the report of public fame. With all humbleness and thankfulness I confess to have received the same of Her Majesty's mere goodness, and more too; for she has made me one of her Privy Council; and, that which was to my greatest comfort, she has allowed me to be one of that most noble Order of the Garter, whereof I have been a Companion, and I am sure the poorest Companion that ever was, now full nineteen years. In these four dignities I have received some indignities, which I would I could as well forget as I can refrain to write of; and thus an end for my public estate: and now a little (dear sir) for my private. Let me with your patience a little trouble you, not for any cause that I find, or you shall see that I have to brag, but rather to show my barrenness, the sooner I do it, for that I hope ere it be long, of friends and old acquaintances we shall be made more than friends, and most loving brothers, in all tender love and loving alliance.

When I was but ten years of age, and a while had been henchman to King Henry the eight[h], I was by that most famous king put to his sweet son Prince Edward, my most dear master, prince and sovereign, the first boy that ever he had; my near kinswoman being his only nurse; my father being his chamberlain, my mother his governess; my aunt by my mother's side in such place as among meaner personages is called a dry nurse, for from the time he left sucking she continually lay in bed with him, so long as he remained in woman's government. As that sweet prince grew in years and discretion, so grew I in favour and liking of him, in such sort as by that time I was twenty-two years old he made me one of the four principal gentlemen of his bed-chamber. While I was present with him he would always be cheerful and pleasant with me, and in my absence give me such words of praise as far exceeded my desert. Sundry times he bountifully rewarded me; finally he always made too much of me: once he sent me into France, and once into Scotland.*
Lastly, not only to my own still felt grief, but also to the universal woe of England, he died in my arms. Within a while after whose death, and after I had spent some months in Spain, neither liking nor liked as I had been, I fancied to live in Ireland, and to serve as Treasurer; and had the

---

* Marginal note: 'N.B.—My going to Spain for the liberty of John, Earl of Warwick, and his brethren.'[122]

Narrative

leading both of horsemen and footmen, and served as ordinarily with them as any other private captain did there, under my brother-in-law the Earl of Sussex, where I served during the reign of Queen Mary and one year after. In which time I had four sundry times, as by letters patent yet appears, the Government of that country, by the name of Lord Justice; thrice by commission out of England, and once by choice of that country; such was the great favour of that Queen to me, and good liking of the people of me.

In the first journey that the Earl of Sussex[123] made, which was a long and great and an honourable one, against James MacConnell [MacDonald], a mighty captain of Scots, whom the Earl of Sussex, after a good fight made with him, defeated and chased him with slaughter of a great number of his best men; I there fought and killed him with my own hand, who thought to have overmatched me. Some more blood I drew, though I cannot brag that I lost any. The second journey the Earl of Sussex made into those quarters of Ulster, he sent me and others into the island of Rathlin, where before, in the time of Sir James Croft's deputation, Sir Ralf Bagenal, Captain [John] Cuffe and others sent by him landed; little to their advantage, for there were they hurt and taken, and the most of their men that landed either killed or taken.[124] But we landed more politiquely and safely, and encamped in the isle until we had spoiled the same of all mankind, corn and cattle in it. Sundry times during my foresaid governments I had sundry skirmishes with the rebels, always with the victory; namely one, and that a great one, which was at the very time that Calais was lost. I at the same time, being Christmas holidays, upon the sudden invaded Fyrkall [*Fercall*], otherwise called O'Molloy's country,[125] the receptacle of all the rebels; burned and wasted the same; and in my return homewards was fought withal by the rebels, the O'Conors, O'Mores and O'Molloys, and the people of Mackgochigan [*MacGeoghegan*], albeit he in person was with me in that skirmish. I received in a frieze jerkin (although armed under it) four or five Irish arrows; some blood I drew with my own hands; but my men beat the rebels well and truly, went through their passes, straits and woods lustily, and killed as many of them as saved not their lives by running away, among whom the chief captain called Callogh O'Molloy was one, and his head brought me by an English gentleman and a good soldier called Robert Cowley.[126] I tarried and encamped in that country till I had cut down and enlarged divers long and strait places, whereby the country ever since has been more obedient and corrigible; somewhat more I did, and so I did as the country well spoke of it, and well judged of it, and I received from the Queen comfortable and thankful letters signed with her own hand, which I have yet to show; and when I was sent to her (as I was once or twice), most graciously she would accept me and my service, and honourably speak of the same, yea and rewarded me.

The rest of my life is with an overlong precedent discourse in part manifested to you, which I humbly and heartily desire you to accept in good part. Some things written may haply be misplaced or mistimed, for help had I none either of any other man, or note of mine, but only such help as my old mother-memory afforded me out of her store. But this to your little comfort I cannot omit, that whereas my father had but one son, and he of no great proof, being of twenty-four years of age at his death, and I having three sons, one of excellent good proof, the second of great good proof, and the third not to be despaired of, but very like, if I die tomorrow next I should leave them worse than my father left me by £20,000, and I am now fifty-four years of age, toothless and trembling, being five thousand pounds in debt,[127] yea and £30,000 worse than I was at the death of my most dear king and master, King Edward the VIth. I have not of the crown of England, of my own getting, so much ground as I can cover with my foot; all my fees amount not to 100 marks [£66] a year; I never had since the Queen's reign any extraordinary aid by licence, forfeit or otherwise; and yet for all that was done, and somewhat more than here is written, I cannot obtain to have in fee farm £100 a year, already in my own possession, paying the rent. *Dura est conditio servorum* [Hard is the servants' lot].

And now, dear Sir and brother, an end of this tragical discourse, tedious for you to read, but more tedious it would have been if it had come written with my own hand as first it was; tragical I may well term

Narrative

it, for that it began with the joyful love and great liking with likelihood of matrimonial match between our most dear and sweet children, whom God bless, and ends with declaration of my unfortunate and hard estate. Our Lord bless you with long life and healthful happiness. I pray you Sir, commend me most heartily to my good Lady cousin and sister your wife, and bless and buss [kiss] our sweet daughter. And if you will vouchsafe, bestow a blessing upon the young knight Sir Philip.

From Ludlow Castle, with more pain than haste, the first of March, 1582 [1583 n.s.].

>Your most assured fast friend and loving brother.
>[*No signature*]

Memorandum to be inserted in some place. A great expedition done by my appointment from Mullengar in West Meath upon Turlogh Lenogh in Tyrone, which made him ever after the more humble. It was done by Sir Nicholas Malby.

Note.—In the wars with Rorie Oge I lay for the most part at Monaster Evan, confronting with the rebel, in which time I hang[ed] a captain of Scots which served under Captain Malby, and all his officers, and I think very near twenty of his men; and by Captain Furrs and his company many or more of them killed, and all for extortions done by him and his people upon the Earl of Ormond in the county of Kilkenny; and yet he still complained he nor his could have no justice of me.

During my abode there I began the bridge of Carlow, over the great river of Barrow, which shortly after was finished to very good purpose.

I built a tower for the guard of the bridge over the great river called the Great or Black Water in Tyrone; the bridge being built by the Earl of Essex. I built and newly erected six or seven several gaols.

De his et de premisis consule [for these and the foregoing matters consult] [Lucas] Dillon, [Nicholas] Malby, [Edward] Waterhouse, [Edmund] Mullineux.[128]

FINIS

[*Separate additional sheet pasted at the front of the MS volume:*]

Note in my first deputation the building of a watermill at Carrickfergus, the repairing and recovering of the great tower in the castle of the same.

The coming to me thither of Sir Arthur Champernoune, Mr John Champernoune, his eldest brother's son and heir, and Mr Philip Butsid and divers other gentlemen, yeomen and seamen of the west of England, desirous to take lands and to inhabit in the north parts of Ireland.[129]

The taking of lands by Sir Thomas Smythe,[130] then Secretary, the possession whereof is held to this day.

Note that Sir Edward Horsey and Sir Thomas Lighton [Leighton] did accompany me and served under my giddon [*guidance*] in sundry of the incursions which I made upon the Arch-rebel Shane O'Neill, who can report the pleasure and profit that is gotten by service in that country.

Abbreviations

BL	British Library, London
SP 63	State Papers, Ireland (Public Record Office, London)
Sidney Letters	*Letters and Memorials of State . . . written and collected by Sir Henry Sidney, Sir Philip Sidney and his brother, Sir Robert Sidney,* ed. Arthur Collins (2 vols, London, 1746)
TCD	Trinity College, Dublin

Notes to Introduction

1. For a detailed discussion of the marriage arrangements between Sir Philip Sidney and Mary Walsingham see Katherine Duncan-Jones, *Sir Philip Sidney: Courtier-Poet* (London, 1991), pp. 224–6; also M. W. Wallace, *The Life of Sir Philip Sidney* (Cambridge, 1915), pp. 280–91.
2. See the Editorial Note, p. 38 above.
3. A good and generally dependable sketch of the whole of Sidney's career is provided by Robert Dunlop in the *Dictionary of National Biography*; detailed discussions of his Irish service are supplied in Nicholas Canny, *The Elizabethan Conquest of Ireland: A Pattern Established, 1565–76*, (Hassocks, 1976), and Ciaran Brady, *The Chief Governors: The Rise and Fall of Reform Government in Tudor Ireland, 1536–1588* (Cambridge, 1994), esp. ch. 3; on his career in Wales see Penry Williams, *The Council in the Marches of Wales under Elizabeth I* (Cardiff, 1958), esp. ch. 12.
4. Sidney to Grey, 17 Sept. 1580: *Sidney Letters*, i, 279–83; Secretary of State Fenton to Leicester, 8 Sept. 1580: SP 63/76/19; Fenton to Walsingham, 5 Nov 1581: SP 63/86/49; Fenton to Leicester, 25 Nov. 1581: SP 63/86/82; Fenton to Burghley, 5 June 1582: SP 63/93/13; Fenton to Burghley, 17 Mar. 1583: SP 63/100/84; see also Auditor Jenyson to Burghley, 15 June 1582: SP 63/88/29; Sir Nicholas Malby to Walsingham, 12 May 1582: SP 63/92/36; Capt. Piers to Walsingham, 11 Apr. 1583, SP 63/101/20..
5. Sidney's 'Notes to be Imparted to Sir Philip Sidney': *Sidney Letters*, i, 295.
6. See his opening comments in the narrative, p. 43.
7. 'A happy place of government it is, for a better people to govern, or better subjects to their Sovereign, Europe holds not' (p. 104).
8. See, for example, 'A Particular Note of Lands, Rents, etc. Secured and Advanced to the Queen by Sir Henry Sidney, 1578': SP 63/64/1; 'A Brief Memorial of Sir Henry Sidney's Service in Ireland' 1578: Lambeth Palace Library, Carew MS 607, ff. 32–3. Similar summaries from Sidney's predecessors in office are scattered throughout the Irish State Papers.

9   Killigrew's manuscript 'Memoir' is in BL, Lansdowne MS 106, no. 31, f. 122; a later version, possibly a redraft by Killigrew himself, is in L. Howard (ed.), *A Collection of Letters* (2 vols, London, 1756), i, 184–8, but a manuscript of this revised piece has not been found.

10 'The Autobiography of Sir James Croft', ed. R. E. Ham, *Institute of Historical Research Bulletin*, no 50 (1977), pp. 48–57.

11 Simon Adams, 'The Patronage of the Crown in Elizabethan Politics: The 1590s in Perspective' in J. A. Guy (ed.), *The Reign of Elizabeth I: Court and Culture in the Last Decade* (Cambridge, 1993), pp. 20–45.

12 See Joan Simon, *Education and Society in Tudor England* (Cambridge, 1966); Kenneth Charlton, *Education in Renaissance England* (London, 1965); J. H Hexter, 'The Education of the Aristocracy in the Renaissance' in his *Reappraisals in History* (London, 1961), pp. 45–70.

13 Though Sidney here seems to regard his return to Ireland in August 1568 as the commencement of a new term in office, in fact his commission as Lord Deputy of 1565 had not been terminated, the question of appointing a successor was never raised, and the order for his return to service was issued in April 1568, a mere eight months after he had left Ireland for court.

14 See Geoffrey Bullough, 'Attitudes to Caesar before Shakespeare' in his *Narrative and Dramatic Sources of Shakespeare*, v: *The Roman Plays* (London, 1964); also T. J. B. Spencer, 'Shakespeare and the Elizabethan Romans', *Shakespeare Survey*, x (1957), pp. 27–38.

15 A useful modern translation which reproduces about half of the massive original and all of the concluding books is provided by Sidney Alexander, *The History of Italy by Francesco Guicciardini* (London, 1969); for Guicciardini's conscious emulation of and departures from the Caesarean model see Felix Gilbert, *Machiavelli and Guicciardini: History and Politics in Renaissance Italy* (Princeton, 1965), ch. 7.

16 *The Historie of Guicciardin* [sic] *reduced into English by Geffray Fenton* (London, 1579); for detailed critical commentary see Rudolf B. Gottfried, *Geoffrey Fenton's 'History of Guicciardin'*, Indiana University Press Humanities Series, no. 3 (Urbana, 1940).

17 *Phillipe de Commynes: Memoirs*, ed. Michael Jones (Harmondsworth, 1972); see esp. Introduction, pp. 11, 35–8, 45–6.

18 English translation: *The Commentaries of Messire Blaize de Montluc, Mareschal of France*, trans. Charles Cotton (London, 1674). A thorough study of the *Commentaries*, their origins and their influence is Paul Corteault, *Blaise de Monluc, Historien: Étude Critique* (Paris, 1908). For the literary context of Monluc's work see R. J. Knecht, 'Military Autobiography in Sixteenth-Century France' in J. R. Mulryne and Margaret Shewring (eds), *War, Literature and the Arts in Sixteenth-Century Europe* (London, 1989). I am grateful to Kenneth Nicholls who first suggested the comparison to me.

19 Monluc, *Commentaries*, chs 1–3.

20 For Sir Philip Sidney's experiences in France at the time of the massacre see James M. Osborne, *The Young Philip Sidney* (New Haven, 1972), pp. 66–73; Wallace, *Sir Philip Sidney*, pp. 120–22.

21 The quotation is from H. F. Hore's brief introduction to his edition in the *Ulster Journal of Archaeology* cited in the Editorial Note. The source-mining of the memoir is a practice from which few modern scholars, myself included, can be exonerated.

22 The chief exponent of this view is Nicholas Canny, who in *The Elizabethan Conquest of Ireland* and related articles identifies Sidney both as a pioneer of new colonising policies and, more importantly, of a new ideological justification for their widespread application.

23 Compare the standard ethnographic commentaries extracted in E. M. Hinton, *Ireland through Tudor Eyes* (New York, 1933) and Andrew Hadfield and John McVeagh (eds), *Strangers To That Land: British Perceptions of Ireland from the Reformation to the Famine* (Gerrards Cross, 1994) and discussed in D. B. Quinn, *The Elizabethans and the Irish* (Ithaca, 1966), where, significantly, Sidney's memoir features only marginally.

24 The most trenchant exponent of this view is Brendan Bradshaw: see his 'The Elizabethans and the Irish', *Studies*, no. 65 (1977), pp. 38–50, and 'The Elizabethans and the Irish: A Muddled Model', *Studies*, no. 70 (1981), pp. 233–44.

25 Compare the silence of the text to Sidney's well-known description and analysis of the state of the Church of Ireland in 1576 in *Sidney Letters*, i, 112–14.

26 This consensus view of Sidney, which I share, is expressed in the standard textbooks: see Colm Lennon, *Sixteenth-Century Ireland: The Incomplete Conquest* (Dublin, 1994), pp. 240–45, and Steven G. Ellis, *Ireland in the Age of the Tudors, 1447–1603: English Expansion and the End of Gaelic Rule* (London, 1998), pp. 304–9.

27 The historian most closely identified with this aspect of Sidney's Irish policy is the present writer: see Brady, *Chief Governors*, pp. 136–58.

28 Tremayne's most important memoranda on this strategy are SP 63/32/64–6; BL Add. MS 48015, ff. 274–9; BL, Cotton MSS, Titus B XII, ff. 357–60.

29 These comments and the following discussion are based upon a systematic review of Sidney's account in the memoir against the extant contemporary correspondence and other materials contained in the State Papers, Ireland (SP 63), the *Calendar of the Carew Manuscripts, 1515–74* (London, 1867), the *Sidney State Papers, 1565–70*, ed. Tomás Ó Laidhin (Irish Manuscripts Commision, Dublin, 1962), the *De Lisle and Dudley Manuscripts*, i–ii (Historical Manuscripts Commission, London, 1925–33), and the herald's account of his campaigns in 1569–70: TCD, MS 660, no. 4.

30 The sittings of the parliament and the sequence of its legislation are carefully traced in Victor Treadwell, 'The Irish Parliament of 1569–71', *Proceedings of the Royal Irish Academy*, lxvi (1966), sect. C, pp. 55–89.

31 Brady, *Chief Governors*, pp. 146–9, 241–4.

32 For Sidney's contemporary justifications of his conduct launched on both theoretical and practical grounds see his 'Instructions to [Edward] Waterhouse', May 1577: *De Lisle and Dudley MSS*, i, 55–6; Sidney to Walsingham, 15 May 1577: BL, Cotton MSS, Titus B X, no. 1; Sidney to Elizabeth I, 20 May 1577: SP 63/58/29; an even more radical defence of his conduct which he may or may not have endorsed was presented at court by his son Philip in his 'Discourse on Irish Affairs' printed in *Miscellaneous Prose of Sir Philip Sidney*, ed. Katherine Duncan-Jones and Jan Van Dorster (Oxford, 1973), pp. 3–12.

33 Ormond had served under the English governor Lord Pelham as governor-general in Munster in 1580; but in December 1582 he was appointed by the English Privy Council as governor of Munster with plenipotentiary powers to bring the rebellion to a close; see his 'Demands' and 'Propositions' and Burghley's endorsements in Nov.–Dec. 1582: SP 63/97/61–3; SP 63/98/35.

34 Throughout the early 1580s leading English administrators in Dublin, including Secretary of State Fenton, Vice-Treasurer Wallop, Sir Warham St Leger, Sir Walter Raleigh and Sir Nicholas Malby, waged a campaign of criticism to undermine Ormond; for a sample see Fenton to Leicester, 8 Dec.1580: SP 63/79/3; Wallop to Walsingham, 23 Apr. 1581: SP 63/82/87; St Leger to Burghley, 3 June 1581: SP 63/83/38; Raleigh to Walsingham, 25 Feb. 1581: SP 63/80/82; Malby to Walsingham, 20 Sept. 1581, SP 63/85/48.

35 Ormond, in any case, knew how to fight back: his special relations with Elizabeth and Burghley ensured that his critics were often themselves the objects of royal displeasure and he himself exonerated: see his 'Demands' and 'Propositions', Nov. 1582: SP 63/97/61–3; and his trenchant reply to criticism to the Privy Council, Oct. 1583: SP 63/105/30, enclosure (i).

36 Sussex's major policy analyses are contained in his memoranda of November 1560 and December 1562: *Calendar of Carew MSS, 1515–74*, pp. 300–4, 330–44.

37 Canny, *Elizabethan Conquest*, ch. 5.

38 See, among several examples, Lord Leonard Grey's list of 'peaces' made, June 1540: *Calendar of Carew MSS, 1515–74*, p. 157; Sussex's 'Memo' on the state of Ireland, Apr. 1562: SP 63/5/101; Sidney's 'A Particular Note of Lands, Rents, etc. Secured and Advanced to the Queen, 1578': SP 63/64/1.

39 See Vincent P. Carey, 'John Derricke's *Image of Irelande*, Sir Henry Sidney, and the Massacre at Mullaghmast, 1578', *Irish Historical Studies*, xxxi (1998–99), pp. 305–27.

40 See, *inter alia*, Irving Ribner, 'Machiavelli and [Philip] Sidney: The *Arcadia* of 1590', *Studies in Philology*, xlvii (1950), pp. 152–72; idem, 'Machiavelli and Sidney's *Discourse to the Queen's Majesty*', *Italica*, xxvi (1949), pp. 117–87; Blair Worden, *The Sound of Virtue: Sir Philip Sidney's 'Arcadia' and Elizabethan Politics* (New Haven, 1996), pp. 29–30, 227–8, 260–63.
41 See in particular Tremayne's tracts in the State Papers: SP 63/32/64–6.
42 For a useful recent synthesis see J. Russell Major, *From Renaissance Monarchy to Absolute Monarchy: French Kings, Nobles and Estates*, (Baltimore, Md., 1994).

Notes to Narrative

1 For details of the complex premarital negotiations between the Sidneys and the Walsinghams see *De Lisle and Dudley MSS*, i, 272–3; the marriage is discussed in its broader context in Wallace, *Sir Philip Sidney*, pp. 280–91.
2 *Spes et fortuna valete*: 'hope and fortune having bid farewell'.
3 Sidney's financial problems were chronic: for an earlier survey of his precarious condition see Sir William Cecil's 'Note on Sir Henry Sidney's Living, 1569': BL, Lansdowne MSS, vol. 10, f. 93; despite his genuine pleas for relief, careful financial and estate management successfully rescued the family from ruin. Evidence that Sidney's circumstances had improved toward the close of his life is supplied by his elaborate funeral arrangements that cost £1,500 and by the substantial inheritance bequeathed to his son and heir Robert. See Lawrence Stone, *The Crisis of the Aristocracy, 1558–1641* (Oxford, 1965), pp. 259, 291–2, 387–8, 540, 784.
4 Shane O'Neill (1529?–67), chief of the O'Neills since 1559 whose demands to be recognised as heir to the earldom of Tyrone, vigorously opposed by the Dublin government, were the source of almost uninterrupted conflict in the 1560s: for further details see Ciaran Brady, *Shane O'Neill* (Dundalk, 1996).
5 Sidney is referring here to the treaty concluded between Conn Bacach O'Neill and Henry VIII in 1542: *Calendar of Carew MSS, 1515–74*, pp. 188–93; for a detailed allocation of the Ulster lordships mentioned in the text see the map by K. W. Nicholls prepared for *A New History of Ireland*, iii: *Early Modern Ireland* (Oxford, 1976), pp. 2–3 and reproduced here (pp. 2–3) by kind permission.
6 Sir Nicholas Bagenal (1508–91), Marshal of the army in Ireland, 1547–56, 1566–90, and planter in Newry since the late 1540s.
7 Calvagh (Callough) O'Donnell (1520?–66), lord of Tír Conaill upon deposing his father Manus in 1555; imprisoned by Shane O'Neill, 1561–63, visited court seeking redress and was granted title to Tír Conaill as earl of Tyrconnell by Elizabeth, but died on his return journey before the patent was issued.

8 For details see *Calendar of Carew MSS, 1515–74*, pp. 373–5.
9 Sidney lists here the principal dynasties of Sligo, Leitrim, east Mayo and part of Roscommon: see map. The settlements concluded in October 1566 are recorded in *Calendar of Carew MSS, 1515–74*, pp. 375–6.
10 Cnoc an Garrán Bán (lit.: White Grove Hill), Co. Sligo.
11 Roscommon Castle, built in 1262, was frequently captured and recaptured throughout the later middle ages by feuding Gaelic Irish and Anglo-Irish families. Refortified by the Great Earl of Kildare in 1499, it fell again to the O'Connors until Sidney reoccupied it in 1566 and placed a garrison there under Thomas Le Strange.
12 Sir Nicholas Malby (1530?–83), serving in Ireland in the midlands and in Ulster from the mid-1550s; appointed President of Connacht by Sidney in 1576 and features prominently in the latter part of the text.
13 Sidney lists here the leading families of Roscommon and east Galway: see map.
14 Though divided by internal feuds, the O'Kellys possessed extensive territories in east Galway; the O'Farrells, equally divided among themselves, were principal lords in Longford; Sidney's final settlement with the O'Farrells is recorded in *Calendar of Carew MSS, 1515–74*, pp. 406–8.
15 Lady Mary Sidney (1530?–86), daughter of John Dudley, Duke of Northumberland, and sister of Robert Dudley, Earl of Leicester, married Sidney in 1554; a formidable figure, deeply conscious of her antecedents, she was a principal lady-in-waiting to Elizabeth in the early years of the reign and contracted the disfiguring smallpox of which Sidney speaks in the text while nursing the queen in 1562, but was later discountenanced by Elizabeth. Despite some strikingly ambivalent references to her in his text (pp. 43, 105), the relationship between the couple remained by all accounts close and affectionate; she survived her husband by two months.
16 Sir Warham St Leger (1525?–97), son of Sir Anthony St Leger, Lord Deputy of Ireland intermittently between 1540 and 1556, was a client of Leicester and Sidney; appointed by Sidney without patent to act as president in Munster in 1566, his promotion was blocked by Elizabeth; having spent much time in Munster in the 1570s, he subsequently acquired substantial lands in the province in the 1580s.
17 Sir Nicholas Heron (d. 1568), soldier resident in Ireland since the mid-1550s; Constable of Leighlin Bridge, 1556–68; sometime Sheriff of Carlow; knighted by Sidney in 1566.
18 Sidney is referring here to the battle at Farsetmore and, as noted in the introduction, has seriously confused the chronology; for a detailed account see G. A. Hayes-McCoy, *Irish Battles* (London, 1965), pp. 68–86. Hugh O'Donnell, a favourite of Sidney's and knighted by him, remained lord of Tír Conaill from 1566 until his deposition by his son Red Hugh (Aodh Ruadh) in 1592.

Notes to Narrative 117

19 A curious piece of mutual mistranslation is on show here: in reporting the Irish messenger's misperception of his family cognisance (crest) emblazoned on his viceregal pennant, Sidney himself misstates the messenger's accurate Gaelic denomination of his banner 'bratach' as 'bracklok'.

20 *Diabolus nunquam dormit*: 'the devil never sleeps' (traditional adage).

21 Thomas Butler, 10th Earl of Ormond (1531–1614), leading Irish noble and Sidney's *bête noir* whose ascendancy over the Irish aristocracy was consolidated by his close personal relations with Queen Elizabeth herself.

22 Gerald FitzGerald, 15th Earl of Desmond (1530?–83), whose difficulty in controlling opposition within his own lordship, combined with the enmity of the earl of Ormond and Queen Elizabeth's inveterate mistrust, forced him into fatal rebellion in 1579–83.

23 John FitzJames FitzGerald (d. 1582), younger brother of Earl Gerald; generally favoured by English administrators in Ireland as a stabilising influence on Desmond until, frustrated by continuous lack of reward, he committed himself irrevocably to rebellion by his assassination of English agents sent to negotiate peace in 1579.

24 Conor O'Brien, 3rd Earl of Thomond (1535?–81); since succeeding to the earldom in 1553 his claims to the whole of Thomond were successfully resisted by other leading O'Briens despite the support of Lord Lieutenant Sussex. Reacting violently against Sidney's attempts to negotiate a settlement by partition, he rose in rebellion in 1570 and fled into exile; he returned on promise of a pardon and in the later 1570s grudgingly accepted a partition of Thomond along the lines proposed by Sidney.

25 Richard Burke, 2nd Earl of Clanrickard (1532?–82), succeeded as earl in 1544 and was generally a supporter of the government until Sidney's plans to introduce a provincial council in Connacht aroused his hostility; was generally believed to be a covert supporter of his sons' rebellion in the late 1570s, but after a spell in the Tower charges against him were dropped and he was allowed to return to his lordship.

26 Robert Cusack (1532?–70), Pale lawyer and since 1561 Second Baron of the Exchequer. Nicholas White (1535?–93), recorder of Waterford, 1564, and Master of the Rolls, 1571–92; a figure of considerable influence in the Dublin administration, he was a close counsellor of the Earl of Ormond and enjoyed unusual favour with Lord Burghley until dismissed from his post following allegations of treason.

27 Alistair MacDonald (d. 1570), chief of the MacDonalds of Kintyre and brother of the MacDonald (MacDonnell) chiefs in Ulster, James and Sorley Boy; responsible for the assassination of Shane O'Neill at Cushendun, he left Ireland shortly afterwards, delegating responsibility for the MacDonnell territories in Antrim to Sorley Boy.

28 William Piers (1510?–1603?), one of the longest-serving soldiers in Ireland; appointed by Sidney as Constable of Carrickfergus in 1566, he remained an extremely influential figure in the politics of Ulster until his retirement to his estate in Westmeath in the 1590s.

29 Sidney's evasive treatment of the death of Shane O'Neill differs considerably from the colourful account first supplied in the act of attainder of O'Neill and popularised by several near-contemporary historians; for the actual circumstances of Shane's death see Ciaran Brady, 'The Killing of Shane O'Neill: Some New Evidence', *Irish Sword*, xv (1982–83), pp. 116–23.

30 Turlough Luineach O'Neill (1531?–95), son of Niall Connallach O'Neill (d. 1544), who was tanist to Conn Bacach; succeeded to the O'Neillship on the assassination of Shane in 1567 and with the aid of Scottish forces supplied by his wife Agnes Campbell successfully overcame internal challenges and the mistrust and occasional hostility of the Dublin government to become by the late 1570s the most powerful Gaelic lord in Ulster.

31 Hugh O'Neill, 3rd Baron of Dungannon and 2nd Earl of Tyrone (1550?–1616); re-established by Sidney in south Ulster in 1568, he survived precariously until the mid-1570s, but gradually developed and consolidated his position in the region; recognised as Earl of Tyrone in 1585 (patent granted, 1587), he joined the Ulster rebellion in 1594; see in general Hiram Morgan, *Tyrone's Rebellion: The Outbreak of the Nine Years War in Tudor Ireland* (Woodbridge, 1993). Sidney's comments here that he had raised young Dungannon may seem to confirm speculations concerning his exposure to English culture at Penshurst and to conflict with evidence that Dungannon actually spent a good part of his youth in Dublin, but the passage may simply imply that Sidney had adopted the young Dungannon during his service in Ireland from 1556 to 1559.

32 Turlough Luineach's submission and acceptance of Sidney's terms on 18 June 1567 are recorded in SP 63/21/28.

33 As Sidney suggests, the MacQuillans were not native Irish, but Cambro-Normans who had come to Ireland in the thirteenth century as clients of the de Burgo earls of Ulster and established a powerful lordship in the Route in Antrim; they rapidly became gaelicised, and by the middle of the sixteenth century they were in rapid decline as a result of intense pressure from the invading MacDonalds.

34 Sidney seems in error here, for Turlough Brasselagh O'Neill was a son not of Conn Bacach but of Conn's son Felim Caoch, who had died in 1542; thus Turlough was a nephew rather than a brother of Shane as Sidney implies; his territory of Clanbrassil stretched between Armagh and the Blackwater.

35 Sidney established the young Hugh O'Neill in the ancient territory of 'the Oneilland', later a barony in Co. Armagh, on Elizabeth's authority: SP 63/23/63.

Notes to Narrative

36 The syntax is confused here but Sidney seems to have the relations generally correct. Conn O'Donnell was the eldest son of the recently deceased chieftain Calvagh (note 7 above), and Hugh who seized the chieftainship against Conn was Calvagh's brother. Until his death in 1583 Conn remained a sworn enemy to Hugh, whom he believed had stolen his birthright.

37 Walter Devereux, 1st Earl of Essex (1539–76); under Queen Elizabeth's authority he initiated in 1572 his 'enterprise of Ulster', a project that aimed at resurrecting a portion of the ancient earldom of Ulster east of the Bann and at expelling the Scots from Ireland. His extraordinary rashness and violence succeeded merely in uniting former enemies among the Scots and the Irish against him and in weakening the position of the English government in Ulster as a whole; he abandoned the project in 1575 and died the following year, possibly of poisoning in revenge for his treacherous murder of the chief of Clandeboy, Brian MacFelim O'Neill.

38 Sir William Fitzwilliam (1529–99) one of the most experienced English officials in Ireland, who served intermittently from 1555 to 1594; Lord Deputy, 1571–5, 1588–94. Relations between Fitzwilliam and Sidney were always strained and became bitter when Fitzwilliam became convinced, not without reason, that Sidney had sought to undermine his first administration. Fitzwilliam's growing reputation for venality led to charges that he was responsible for driving the Ulster lords into rebellion in the 1590s.

39 The chieftains listed here were all presented at court by Sidney between December 1567 and February 1568: see the settlements and arrangements recorded in SP 63/22/60, 65 and SP 63/23/12, 17, 19, 51, 56–8.

40 *Foris triumpho at domi plero*: 'triumph abroad but ridicule at home'. Despite Sidney's hint, no single originator of the phrase has been traced in the standard concordances and dictionaries; the contrasting juxtaposition of *foris* and *domus* was a commonplace in late Latin writers.

41 Agnes Campbell (*c.* 1540–90), Scottish noblewoman, sister of the 6th earl of Argyll; married Turlough Luineach O'Neill in 1569 and played a crucial role in bolstering his military strength while using her renowned diplomatic skills to broker several peaces on his behalf with both the MacDonnells and the Dublin government.

42 Sidney lists here the principal families of Co. Down: Magennis's country was named Iveagh; Kylwarlin (Culverin), Kylultagh and the Ards peninsula were largely inhabited by semi-autonomous branches of the O'Neills.

43 James FitzMaurice FitzGerald (d. 1579), a principal military officer in the Desmond lordship. FitzMaurice rose in rebellion in 1568, ostensibly to defend the earldom following Sidney's arrest of Desmond and sustained his rebellion until Desmond's restoration in 1573. Fled into exile in 1575 with aim of gathering a major invasion force to raise a general rebellion against the English in

Ireland, returned with a very small force in July 1579, and was killed in a skirmish shortly afterwards.

44 Sidney is referring here to the sudden displacement as governor and execution for treason of Thomas, 8th earl of Desmond, in 1468 by the English Justiciar, John Tiptoft, Earl of Worcester; the action was widely regarded as a scandal in Ireland, and the response of the Geraldine alliance forced Edward IV to recognise FitzGerald influence by nominating Desmond's cousin and brother-in-law, Thomas, 7th Earl of Kildare, as governor in 1471.

45 Sir Edmund Butler (1534–1603?), brother of the earl and next in line; though pardoned for his activities in the rebellion, Sir Edmund was never restored in blood; for further details of the rebellion described here by Sidney see David Edwards, 'The Butler Revolt of 1569', *Irish Historical Studies*, xxviii (1992–93), pp. 228–55.

46 Sir Edward Fitton (1527–79), appointed Lord President of Connacht in 1569, a post he held without distinction but under difficult circumstances; he abandoned the post in 1572, but remained a member of the Irish Council; appointed Vice-Treasurer and Treasurer at Wars in 1575.

47 The figures listed here are Gaelic families of south Kerry and west Cork, semi-autonomous of the MacCarthy More (see note 54 below); for contemporary evidence of their activities in the rebellion see SP 63/26/4, enclosure (ix).

48 Sir Peter Carew (1514–75), adventurer who, on the basis of ancient documents, came to Ireland in 1568 to lay claim to several parcels of land. His activities were said to have been a major cause of the Butler revolt of 1569, but Carew also exploited anti-Ormondite sentiment among the Gaelic Irish of Leinster to establish an alternative support base.

49 Sir Barnaby FitzPatrick, 2nd Baron of Upper Ossory (1535?–81), son of the Gaelic lord Mac Giolla Pádraig; brought to court early and was a page (and reputedly whipping-boy) of Edward VI; returned to Ireland in the mid-1550s and succeeded his father as baron in 1576.

50 For Lady Ursula St Leger's personal contemporary account of the affair see SP 63/28/38.

51 Edmund Tremayne (d. 1582) came to Ireland as special commissioner of Secretary of State Sir William Cecil in 1569; composed several important memoranda of Irish policy in the early 1570s and appears to have acted as personal adviser to Sidney at that time.

52 Earthmound: from the Irish *Oir Mumhain*: East Munster. The claim of the gentlemen that they were of more ancient settlement 'than any Butler is' and that they had been 'given away' to the Butlers shows at once a remarkably live sense of early colonial history on their part (the Ormond palatinate was not in fact established until the reign of Edward III, long after the territory of Tipperary had been settled

by the colonials and shired) and a continuing sense of independence from the Butler house; however, we have only Sidney's word for this reported speech.

53 Sidney had adopted the Dudley crest of the ragged staff as his own cognisance upon his marriage to Lady Mary Dudley, so the inference of the Butlers, on this ground at any rate, was far from unreasonable.

54 Donal MacCarthy More, 1st Earl of Clancare (d. 1597), lord of extensive territories in south Kerry; created earl in 1565, he continued to support the Crown until alienated by the Munster plantation in the 1580s; he died in rebellion.

55 Edward Butler (1540?–1603?), younger brother of the Earl of Ormond and reputedly the most unruly of his siblings; narrowly escaped execution for his part in the 1569 revolt and was never restored in blood.

56 Sir Thomas Cusack (1490–1571), Pale lawyer and a figure of major influence in the Dublin government since the 1530s; is credited with being a principal author of the conciliatory policy of 'surrender and regrant' in the 1540s; Lord Chancellor 1546–55, he was Sidney's choice again for the office in 1565, but Elizabeth refused to confirm him; suspected of being too partial to the house of Kildare, he gradually lost influence.

57 Sir Lucas Dillon (1530?–92), Pale lawyer and administrator; Attorney General, 1566; Chief Baron of the Exchequer, 1570. An especial favourite of Sidney, who knighted him, Dillon was nevertheless a committed Catholic who refused to attend official church services and turned down the offer of promotion to the lord chancellorship probably owing to the requirement of taking the oath of allegiance.

58 The White Knight, Thomas FitzGibbon (d. 1570); died in rebellion and attained posthumously in 1571; his lands in Co. Kerry were subsequently estimated as worth a seigniory and a half and were confiscated by the act of attainder in 1571, but confiscation was not effected until the 1590s.

59 A detailed contemporary report of the expedition by Sidney's herald records that while Sidney was responsible for the destruction of 'the new castle', Captain Collier and others were responsible for the siege and capture of 'the old castle': TCD, MS 660, no. 4.

60 Kerrycurrihy, a barony in west Cork which was the main inheritance of James FitzMaurice FitzGerald; his dispossession by Sir Warham St Leger in 1566, done with approval of the Earl of Desmond himself, was a major cause of his rebellion in 1568. Its principal castle, Carrigaline, was a large fortification built by the Anglo-Norman de Cogans in the thirteenth century.

61 Sir Maurice FitzGerald, 1st Viscount Decies (d. 1574), successfully resisted traditional claims of the Earl of Desmond to overlordship of his land in the Decies, Co. Waterford, by seeking the protection of the Earl of Ormond. His creation as Viscount Decies by Elizabeth in 1568 effectively suppressed Desmond's title to the area. His brother James succeeded to the title on his death.

62   Richard Lord Power, Baron of Curraghmore, Co. Waterford (1520?–88); succeeded to the title on his brother's death in royal service at Calais. Though strongly gaelicised, and sworn enemies of the citizens of Waterford, the family through the protection of the Earl of Ormond steadily increased its fortunes over the sixteenth century.

63   Sir William Burke a representative of an Anglo-Norman family long settled around Castleconnell, Co. Limerick. As with Sir Maurice FitzGerald and Lord Power, he was greatly aided in sustaining his independence of his Desmond overlord by the protection of the Earl of Ormond and was raised to the peerage by Elizabeth as 1st Baron Castleconnell in 1580.

64   Rory MacShee (d. *c.* 1598). The MacShees were the traditional galloglas of the Desmond earls; MacShee's pardon is recorded in the *The Irish Fiants of the Tudor Sovereigns: Elizabeth,* no. 2274. MacShee joined with Desmond in rebellion in 1579, but surrendered on terms the following year. He may be the same Rory MacShee who played a leading role in the insurrection against the plantation in the late 1590s.

65   Sir Humphrey Gilbert (1539?–83), Elizabethan adventurer and colonial projector whose ruthless conduct during his brief service as colonel in Munster (1569–70) rendered him notorious in Ireland. Though he devised several colonial projects for Ireland, he did not live to see any come to fruition.

66   Sir John Perrot (1527?–92), Lord President of Munster, 1571–73; Lord Deputy, 1584–88; a highly energetic and ambitious administrator. The rashness which was to characterise his years as viceroy is perhaps foreshadowed during his service in Munster in his challenge to the rebel James FitzMaurice to meet him in single combat.

67   Thomas Stukely (d. 1578), Elizabethan soldier and adventurer, a client of Sidney's. His ambitions for a career in Ireland were blocked by allegations of piracy and corruption; discountenanced by the English government, Stukely soldiered abroad and helped raise a force for FitzMaurice which he diverted (fatally for him) to service in north Africa.

68   Ralph Rokeby (1527?–96), lawyer; briefly Chief Justice in Connacht under Sir Edward Fitton in 1570, but returned to his legal career in London in 1572.

69   Patrick Sherlock (*fl.* 1560s–70s), scion of an ancient Anglo-Norman Waterford family; a somewhat shadowy figure; a client of the Earl of Ormond, he nonetheless commanded respect from Sidney and others; he was the author of a number of tracts concerning the reform of Munster.

70   Sidney presents a somewhat biased view of the two Teige O'Briens: Teige MacMurrough was the son of the 1st Earl of Thomond; his first cousin Teige MacConor was the son of the previous chieftain. Both had reason to believe that the 3rd Earl, Conor, had usurped their birthrights.

Notes to Narrative 123

71 *Jura regalia*: 'rights of kingship', i.e. regalities.
72 Kedagh (or Cadogh) O'More was killed by his own kinsman Donal MacCahir O'More in 1548; his sons Lysagh and Cahir became principal leaders of native resistance to the plantation of Laois in the 1560s. Sidney's contemporary report of the executions was made in May 1570: SP 63/30/52.
73 Hugh MacShane O'Byrne (d. 1580), chief of the O'Byrnes, who controlled much of eastern and southern Wicklow. Among his children mentioned by Sidney may have been his heir and successor, Feagh MacHugh.
74 Sidney's boast is valid: *The Statutes from the Tenth Year of King Henry VI to the Thirteenth Year of our Most Gracious and Sovereign Lady, Queen Elizabeth, Made and Established in Her Highness' Realm of Ireland* (London, 1572) was the product of a commission established and in part subvented by him in 1569; much in use until the 1630s, only one copy appears to have survived (in the Bradshaw Collection, Cambridge University Library).
75 13 Eliz. I, c. 1: *Irish Statutes* (1786 ed.), i, 376.
76 Sir William Gerrard (1528–81), having served with Sidney in Wales, was appointed Lord Chancellor on Sidney's nomination in 1576. His differences with Sidney are amply discussed later in the text.
77 11 Eliz. I, sess. 4, c. 1: *Irish Statutes* (1786 ed.), i, 353.
78 The contemporary record reveals that it was the Earl of Ormond rather than Sidney who seized and placed garrisons in Thomond's castles: see SP 63/30/67.
79 Sorley Boy MacDonald (MacDonnell in Ireland) (1505?–90), chief of the MacDonnells in Antrim after the death at the hands of Shane O'Neill of his brother James. Survived several ferocious attacks on his settlement, especially the massacre perpetrated by the Earl of Essex in 1575, and eventually secured tenurial recognition and rights of denization from Lord Deputy Perrot in 1586.
80 Sir John Norris (1547?–97), Elizabethan soldier and adventurer who came to Ireland with Essex in 1572 and, following several army commissions in Ireland and elsewhere, was made Lord President of Munster in 1584, but was largely an absentee, delegating responsibility to his brother Thomas.
81 'Petitions of Turlough Luineach O'Neill', 3 Nov. 1575: SP 63/53/56. This would appear to be another side-swipe at Essex; the claim to have overlordship of Maguire, conceded by Essex, had never been granted acceptable and was not allowed by Sidney.
82 James MacConnell MacDonald (d. 1565), chief of the MacDonalds of the Isles, spearheaded MacDonald expansion into Ulster in the 1550s, was captured by Shane after the battle of Glentaisie (1565), and died while in captivity.
83 Sidney lists here the leading Gaelic and gaelicised families of the west midlands and Ossory; the adoption of the Gaelic 'Sionnach' ('Shenogh' in the text) by the

Anglo-Norman Foxes is a particularly clear illustration of the extent of this family's gaelicisation.

84 Henry Davells (d. 1579), long-serving English soldier in Leinster and Munster; Constable of Leighlin Bridge as deputy to Nicholas Heron, Constable of Dungarvan, in 1570; he was frequently employed on delicate diplomatic missions among the disaffected Munster lords, on the last of which he was murdered in his bed by the rebel Sir John of Desmond.

85 James FitzRichard, 1st Viscount Barry (d. 1581); a violent man who seized the barony of Buttevant by the murder of most of his rivals, he was nevertheless supported by the Crown because of his opposition to the Earl of Desmond; created viscount in 1568, though his actions and motives remained suspect, he continued in his allegiance even after the outbreak of the Desmond rebellion in 1579.

86 Condon: ancient Anglo-Norman family (originally Caunteton) long settled in Co. Cork in the territory surrounding Cregg Castle, traditionally known as Condon's country; the territory was resumed by the Crown on the attainder of Patrick Condon in 1575.

87 Imokilly: barony in south-west Cork: see map; the seneschal, John FitzEdmund FitzGerald (not FitzGibbon as Sidney seems to imply) (d. 1589), though a staunch ally of James FitzMaurice FitzGerald in both of his rebellions, managed to negotiate a pardon in the 1580s and died in possession of his lands.

88 David Roche (1530?–82), accounted 1st Viscount Roche of Fermoy; though knighted by Sidney in 1567, no record of the viscountcy survives, but he was acknowledeged to have held the title as early as 1575.

89 The lands of the Knight of the Valley or Knight of the Glen (Glyn) were in Glyn and Kenry, Co. Limerick. Sir Thomas FitzJohn was attainted posthumously in the parliament of 1569–71, but his grandson Edmund successfully sued for a restoration.

90 *Salvo suo ordine*: 'on the validity of their ordination'. This is a fascinating encounter that is not recorded elsewhere; it reveals that as late as 1576, six years after the papal bull excommunicating Elizabeth, some Irish bishops were still hoping for a reconciliation. The issue dividing them from Sidney centred upon the apostolic succession: while they were apparently willing to surrender their temporalities (lands, revenues, etc.) and have them regranted *de novo* by Elizabeth, they would not surrender the spiritual titles granted them by the pope in order to be reinstalled by Elizabeth acting in her capacity as Supreme Governor of the Church of Ireland.

91 These are identified in a contemporary report by the Earl of Ormond as Mahon and Donough O'Brien, sons of Murrough O'Brien, Bishop of Killaloe: SP 63/30/56, enclosure (iii).

92 O'Shaughnessy's country straddling the borders between Galway and Clare (see map); the Elizabethan chief, Sir Dermot, successfully established independence

of the Earls of Clanrickard and Thomond by securing the surrender and regrant of his possessions under the Crown in 1569.

93 Sidney lists here the principal vassal families of the MacWilliam Burke of Mayo (currently Shane MacOliver (d. 1580); yet despite his accuracy in deriving the English origins of the families mentioned, he appears to perpetrate a significant phonetic confusion: the Mac William Uachtar (Eughter), or Upper MacWilliam, was in fact the Gaelic denomination of the Burkes of Clanrickard; the denomination of the Mayo Burkes was Mac William Iochtar, or Lower MacWilliam; but given the clash between geography and language Sidney's error is at once understandable and suggestive also of his hazy absorption of Gaelic terms.

94 Ulick (d. 1601) and John (d. 1583) Burke, first and second sons of the 2nd Earl of Clanrickard. Though they continued in alliance throughout the 1570s, the ever-present tensions between them broke out on their father's death (1582), after which Ulick murdered John (possibly with the connivance of the Connacht President, Sir Nicholas Malby) and was recognised as 3rd Earl of Clanrickard; a third son, William, was executed for treason by Malby in 1581.

95 Possibly John FitzJames Lynch, Church of Ireland Bishop of Elphin, 1583–1611.

96 *In odium tertie nempe*: 'in [common] hatred of a third party, of course': i.e. the English government.

97 MacHugh and Mac Redmond were gaelicised vassals of the Clanrickard Burkes.

98 Grace O'Malley (Granuaile) (*c.* 1530–1603), a remarkable political woman of her time. Daughter of the chief of the O'Malleys, she married first into the O'Flahertys and then to the *tánaiste* of the MacWilliam Burke of Mayo (see notes 93 and 99); for further details see Anne Chambers, *Granuaile: The Life and Times of Grace O'Malley, 1530–1603* (Dublin, 1979).

99 Richard in Iarainn [Richard in Iron] Burke (d. 1583); though *tánaiste* to Shane (Sir John) MacOliver as MacWilliam Burke of Mayo, Richard succeeded to the title in 1581 only after intense competition with his uncle Richard MacOliver; he was strongly supported by Sir Nicholas Malby, who knighted him on his accession.

100 For Sidney's contemporary record of these events dated June 1576 and his restoration of the castle of Ibarrye see SP 63/57/5.

101 Royal commission to hear and determine (judge) civil and criminal cases according to the procedures of common law.

102 Thomas Masterson (d. 1590?), English servitor principally in Leinster since the mid-1550s; Constable and Seneschal of Wexford, 1570; Constable of Ferns, 1583; acquired substantial estates in Wexford.

103 Richard Synnott of Ballybrenan, Co. Wexford; his seneschalship of the MacMurroughs' country was never confirmed by patent.

104 Francis Agard (d. 1577), highly experienced and influential soldier and administrator, holding office since 1553 as Constable of Ferns; a member of the Irish

Council since the mid-1550s; seneschal of the O'Byrnes' and O'Tooles' countries until his death; he was unusual in being a figure repected by both the English administration, the community of the Pale, and the Gaelic Irish Lords.

105 Christopher Nugent, 9th Baron Delvin (1538?–1602), prominent in the opposition to Sidney's plans to introduce a composition tax in the Pale in lieu of military exactions; he was also a political ally of the 11th Earl of Kildare. Narrowly escaping a treason trial following the rising in the Pale in 1580, he remained a highly suspect figure thereafter because of his Catholicism, but he proved his loyalty during the Nine Years War.

106 Nicholas Nugent (c. 1538–82), grandson of Richard, 7th Baron Delvin; principal solicitor, 1566; Second Baron of the Exchequer, 1570. Extremely active in the agitation against Sidney's composition in 1576–77, he was nonetheless appointed Chief Justice of the Common Pleas in 1580 on the recommendation of Chancellor Gerrard. Implicated in the rising in the Pale in 1580, he was summarily tried and executed in 1582, victim of a vendetta of his old rival the Chief Justice of Queen's Bench, Sir Robert Dillon (see note 109 below).

107 On Sidney's plan to commute the cess by means of a 'composition', and the hostile reaction of the Pale to his proposals, see Ciaran Brady, 'Conservative Subversives: The Community of the Pale and the Dublin Administration, 1556–1586' in P. J. Corish (ed.), *Radical, Rebels and Establishments: Historical Studies XV* (Belfast, 1995), pp. 11–32.

108 Henry Burnell (c. 1540–1614), Richard Netterville (1547–1607) and Barnaby Scurlock (1520 – after 1586): Sidney names here the principal leaders of the opposition in the English Pale both to the multiple exactions of the English garrison (the cess) and to Sidney's attempts in 1575–77 to reform the cess by the introduction of a non-parliamentary tax (composition). Scurlock had been active in the protest against the army since the 1550s, when he was dismissed from his post as Attorney General; Netterville and Burnell were prominent among the law students who made representations against Lord Lieutenant Sussex in 1561. All were alleged to be recusants; both Netterville and Burnell were allied with the Earl of Kildare; Burnell was briefly Third Justice of Queen's Bench in the late 1590s

109 Sir Robert Dillon (d. 1597), a member of a leading Pale family in Co. Meath; remained loyal to the Crown and was unusual among Palesmen in embracing the Reformation; second justice in Connacht, 1570; Chancellor of the Exchequer, 1572; Chief Justice of Queen's Bench, 1580. Dillon was ruthless in the suppression of insurrection in the Pale; his conduct at that time was the cause of serious allegations made against him in the Pale in the 1590s and his temporary removal from the bench in 1593; he was restored in 1595.

110 Rory Oge O'More (d. 1577), son of a former chief of the O'Mores; at one time protected and encouraged by Francis Cosby and some other major planters in

Laois (Queen's County), but by the early 1570s had established himself as an indepenent force in the territory; though he submitted to Sidney in 1575, he was again leading a major rebellion in alliance with the dispossessed O'Connors of Offaly (King's County) in 1577.

111 Sir Henry Harrington (1567–1605), planter and administrator; in Ireland since the mid-1570s; seneschal of the O'Byrnes' and O'Tooles' countries, 1577, succeeding Francis Agard; acquired considerable estates for himself in Leinster. Appointed to the Irish Council in the early 1580s, he remained an influential and controversial member of the Dublin government throughout the 1590s and early 1600s.

112 Robert Harpoole (or Hartpole) (d. 1594), soldier; in Ireland since the mid-1550s, when he was deputy constable at Leighlin Bridge; Constable of Carlow, 1567; acquired a substantial plantation holding in Laois (Queen's County); married into the FitzGeralds of Kildare.

113 Cormac O'Connor: Sidney seems to be somewhat confused here: Cormac O'Connor, son of Brian (formerly the O'Connor Faly), did indeed flee to Scotland in 1550, secured a pardon from Elizabeth, and returned under licence in the 1560s; but the figure who rose out with Rorie Oge O'More in 1576 is recorded in contemporary reports as Cormac MacCormac, a son of the figure described by Sidney.

114 Sir William Drury (1527–79), long-serving professional soldier, mostly as commander of the garrison at Berwick; came to Ireland with Sidney in 1575; appointed President of Munster in 1576 and after difficult beginnings appeared to have established good relations with Desmond. Appointed Lord Justice after Sidney's recall, he died while on campaign in the early days of the Desmond rebellion.

115 Sir Edward Waterhouse (1535–91), long-serving secretary to Sidney and informal clerk of the Irish Council; appointed receiver general of the Irish revenues, 1579; Chancellor of the Irish Exchequer, 1586; obtained substantial lands in Leinster, but apparently as a speculation, as he shortly sold on the bulk of his Irish estates.

116 MacMahon's country: Co. Monaghan. The conflict which Sidney sought to punish was, according to the contemporary records, a major one in which over twenty of the young gentlemen of the Pale were killed: see Malby to Sidney, 3 May 1578: SP 63/60/55. Despite Sidney's raid, Art MacMahon had still not made restitution by the time of his death in 1579.

117 Sir Hugh Magennis was seeking official retribution after Sidney's departure: SP 63/64/116.

118 *Secundum jus talionis*: retributive justice, i.e. 'an eye for an eye', etc.

119 The white rod was the ceremonial staff of the Lord Chancellor.

120 Psalm cii, 6: 'I am become like a pelican in the wilderness: and like an owl (*nicticorax*) that is in the desert'.

121 See *Sidney Letters*, i, 247–50.

122 The John Dudley referred to in this highly compressed reference is not the Earl of Warwick and Duke of Northumberland executed for treason by Queen Mary in November 1553, but his son John (d. 1554), who held the title Warwick as a courtesy during his father's lifetime and who was placed under arrest in Sidney's care following Northumberland's execution. What Sidney appears to be intimating here is that his purpose in joining the diplomatic mission of the Earl of Bedford and the Earl of Sussex to Spain to negotiate the queen's marriage had been to gain sufficient credit with the new regime to plead for the release of John and his siblings Amyas and Robert, which he did successfully on his return. His own account of his motives contrasts interestingly with the speculation of some historians that he went to Spain to absorb the new colonial ideology.

123 Thomas Radcliffe, 3rd Earl of Sussex (1526–83), viceroy in Ireland, 1556–65. Sidney came to Ireland with Sussex, but differences over court politics, through Sidney's alliance with Sussex's rival Leicester and Irish policy, led to a serious estrangement; Sidney believed with reason that Sussex had done much to undermine him during his first administration.

124 For a contemporary account of the débâcle see Sir Thomas Cusack to the Earl of Warwick, 27 Sept. 1551: SP 61/3/52.

125 Sidney's contemporary account is Sidney to Sussex, 26 Feb. 1558: SP 62/2/14, where his principal emphasis was on the cutting of passes to gain better entry to the midlands.

126 This Robert Cowley (d. 1573) may have been related to the Cowleys of Kilkenny, clients of the house of Ormond and government officers (a Robert Cowley was Master of the Rolls in the 1530s); but his profession and Sidney's emphasis on his Englishness suggests that he may be related to Anthony Colly, a soldier serving with Sir William Skeffington in 1532. He was killed in action against the O'Mores.

127 Elsewhere Sidney estimated that he had accumulated debts in excess of £10,000 through his Irish service: see 'Notes of Lands, Woods, Leases, etc. sold', 1578: SP 63/64/18.

128 Edmund Molyneaux (d. after 1587), Sidney's personal secretary and retainer; sometime clerk of the Irish Council.

129 The Champernoune project never got beyond initial prospectings: see Cecil to Sidney, 27 July 1567: SP 63/21/64.

130 Sir Thomas Smith (1513–77), scholar and Secretary of State, 1572; secured licence to establish an experimental colony in the Ards peninsula (Co. Down), which failed upon the killing of his son Thomas: see D. B. Quinn, 'Sir Thomas Smith and the Beginnings of English Colonial Theory', *Procedings of the American Philosophical Society*, lxxxix (1945), pp. 543–60; Hiram Morgan, 'The Colonial Venture of Sir Thomas Smith', *Historical Journal*, xxviii (1985), pp. 261–78.

Bibliography

Adams, Simon, 'The Patronage of the Crown in Elizabethan Politics: The 1590s in Perspective' in J. A. Guy (ed.), *The Reign of Elizabeth I: Court and Culture in the Last Decade* (Cambridge, 1993), pp. 20–45

Bradshaw, Brendan, 'The Elizabethans and the Irish', *Studies*, no. 65 (1977), pp. 38–50

—— 'The Elizabethans and the Irish: A Muddled Model', *Studies*, no. 70 (1981), pp. 233–44

Brady, Ciaran, 'Court, Castle and Country: The Framework of Government in Tudor Ireland' in Ciaran Brady and Raymond Gillespie (eds), *Natives and Newcomers: Essays on the Making of Irish Colonial Society, 1534–1641* (Dublin, 1986), pp. 22–49

—— *The Chief Governors: The Rise and Fall of Reform Government in Tudor Ireland, 1536–1588* (Cambridge, 1994)

Canny, Nicholas, 'The Ideology of Colonization: from Ireland to America' in *William and Mary Quarterly*, xxx (1973), pp. 575–98

—— *The Elizabethan Conquest of Ireland: A Pattern Established, 1565–76* (Hassocks, 1976)

—— *From Reformation to Restoration: Ireland, 1534–1660* (Dublin, 1987)

Carey, Vincent P., 'John Derricke's *Image of Irelande*, Sir Henry Sidney, and the Massacre at Mullaghmast, 1578', *Irish Historical Studies*, xxxi (1998–99), pp. 305–27

Crawford, Jon G., *Anglicising the Government of Ireland: The Irish Privy Council and the Expansion of Tudor Rule* (Dublin, 1993)

Dunlop, Robert, 'Sidney, Henry' in *Dictionary of National Biography*

Edwards, David, 'The Butler Revolt of 1569', *Irish Historical Studies*, xxviii (1992–93), pp. 228–55

Ellis, Steven G., *Ireland in the Age of the Tudors, 1447–1603: English Expansion and the End of Gaelic Rule* (London, 1998)

Guy, J. A., *Tudor England* (2nd ed., Oxford, 1997)

Knecht, R. J., 'Military Autobiography in Sixteenth-Century France' in J. R. Mulryne and Margaret Shewring (eds), *War, Literature and the Arts in Sixteenth-Century Europe* (London, 1989)

Lennon, Colm, *Sixteenth-Century Ireland: The Incomplete Conquest* (Dublin, 1994)

Nicholls, Kenneth, *Gaelic and Gaelicised Ireland in the Later Middle Ages* (Dublin, 1972)

Osborne, James M., *The Young Philip Sidney* (New Haven, 1972)

Treadwell, Victor, 'The Irish Parliament of 1569–71', *Proceedings of the Royal Irish Academy*, lxvi (1966), sect. C, pp. 55–89

Williams, Penry, *The Council in the Marches of Wales under Elizabeth I* (Cardiff, 1958)

—— *The Tudor Regime* (Oxford, 1979)

Worden, Blair, *The Sound of Virtue: Philip Sidney's 'Arcadia' and Elizabethan Politics* (New Haven, 1992)

Index

Adams, Simon, 7
Agard, Francis, 92, 125–6, 127
Alexander, Sidney, 112
Armagh, 75, 83
Arnold, Sir Nicholas, 5
Athenry, 89
Athlone, 47–8, 88
Aylward, Piers, 65

Bagenal, Sir Nicholas, 44, 55, 83, 94
Bagenal, Sir Ralph, 107
Ballinasloe, 90–1
Barnewall, Christopher, 93
Barry, James FitzRichard, first Viscount, 16, 50, 68, 70, 85, 124
Beleek Castle, 46
Boyle Abbey, 47
Bradshaw, Brendan, 113
Brady, Ciaran, 111, 113, 114, 115, 118, 126
Brady, Hugh, 60
Bullough, Geoffrey, 112
Burghley, Lord, 103, 114, 117
Burke, John, 87–8, 125
Burke, Richard, *see* Clanrickard, Earl of
Burke, Richard in Iarainn (in Iron), 90
Burke, Ulick, 87–8, 125
Burke, Sir William, 72, 122
Burnell, Henry, 95, 126
Butler, Sir Edmund, 62–4, 65–6, 75, 79, 120
  escape from Dublin Castle, 77
Butler, Edward, 66–7, 121
Butler, Lord James, 63

Butler, Sir Theobald, 63, 70
Butler, Thomas, *see* Ormond, Earl of
Butsid, Philip, 110
Buttevant, 70

Caesar, memoirs compared to Sidney's, 8–9, 10
Campbell, Agnes, 15, 30, 59, 75–6, 118, 119
Canny, Nicholas, 111, 113, 114
Carew, Sir Peter, 63, 120
Carey, Vincent, 39, 114
Carlow, 76, 109
Carrickfergus, 13–14, 44, 56, 59–61, 82, 83, 110
Carrigaline, 70, 121
Casimir, Duke John, 104
Castle Barry, 90
Cavanaghs, 88–9
Cecil, Sir William, 115, 120
Chambers, Anne, 125
Champernoune, Sir Arthur, 13, 110
Champernoune, John, 13, 110
Charlton, Kenneth, 112
Cheston, Captain Thomas, 70
Clancare, Donal MacCarthy More, first Earl of, 31, 63, 66, 70, 79–80, 85, 121
Clanrickard, Richard Burke, second Earl of, 25, 52, 87, 88, 89, 102–3, 117
Clonmel, 64–5
Collier, William, 33, 63–4, 69–70, 74, 89, 100, 121
Colly, Anthony, 128

Index

Comerford, 78
Commines, Phillippe de, 10
composition tax, 17, 19–20, 22–3, 32–3, 92–6, 126
Condon, Patrick, 124
Condons, 50, 85, 124
Corish, P.J., 126
Cork, 64, 70–1, 84
Corteault, Paul, 112
Cosby, Francis, 126
Courcy, Lord, 50, 85
Cowley, Robert, 108, 128
coyne and livery, 28–9, 62
Croft, Sir James, 7, 8, 107
Cuffe, John, 107
Cusack, Patrick, 74
Cusack, Robert, 52
Cusack, Sir Thomas, 67, 121, 128

Davells, Henry, 16, 84, 124
Decies, Sir Maurice FitzGerald, first Viscount, 71, 121, 122
Delvin, Christopher Nugent, ninth Baron, 92–3
Derricke, John, *Image of Irelande*, 34
Derry, 48
Desmond, Gerald FitzGerald, fifteenth Earl of, 16, 49–52, 58, 70, 85, 99
Desmond, Sir John of, 16–17, 25, 33, 50, 51–2, 57, 58, 61–2, 84, 117
Devereux, Walter, *see* Essex, Earl of
Dillon, Sir Lucas, 17, 67–8, 76, 92, 96, 109, 121
Dillon, Sir Robert, 96, 126
Donegal, 45
Drogheda, 48, 73, 82
Drury, Sir William, 99, 101, 102, 127
Dublin Castle, 77

Dudley, John, Duke of Northumberland, 4, 116
Dudley, John (Northumberland's son), 106, 128
Dudley, Mary, *see* Sidney, Lady Mary
Dudley, Lord Robert, 5, 116
Duncan-Jones, Katherine, 111, 114
Dungarven, 84
Dunlop, Robert, 111

Edward, Prince, 106
Edwards, David, 120
Eliott, Thomas, 86
Elizabeth I, Queen of England, 1, 6, 7, 43–4, 115, 116
Ellis, Steven G., 113
Enniscorthy, 62
Essex, Walter Devereux, first Earl of, 13–14, 25, 29, 30, 56, 60, 78, 82, 83, 90, 99, 109, 119, 123

Farneys, 44
Farsetmore, 21, 48, 116
Fenton, Geoffrey, 10, 114
Fitton, Sir Edward, 19, 63, 73, 74, 94, 103, 120, 122
FitzGerald, Gerald, *see* Desmond, Earl of
FitzGerald, Sir James, 84
FitzGerald, John FitzEdmund, 85–6, 124
FitzGerald, John FitzJames, *see* Desmond, John of
FitzGerald, Sir Maurice, *see* Decies, Viscount
FitzGerald, Thomas FitzJames, 61
FitzGibbon, Thomas (the White Knight), 68, 69, 70, 78, 121

FitzJohn, Sir Thomas, 124
FitzMaurice, James, 17, 58, 61–2, 63, 64, 68, 69, 70–1, 72–3, 119–20, 121, 124
FitzMaurice, Patrick, 57
FitzMaurice, Thomas, 57
FitzPatrick, Sir Barnaby (Baron of Upper Ossary), 14, 33, 34, 64, 76, 93, 100–1, 120
FitzRichard, James, *see* Barry, Viscount
Fitzwilliam, Sir William, 56, 119
Fleming, James, 93
Foxes, 84
Furres, Captain, 100, 109

Galway, 87–8
Geraldines, 29, 63, 68–9, 71, 85
Gerrard, Sir William, 25–6, 29, 30, 79, 93, 96, 102, 123, 126
Gilbert, Felix, 112
Gilbert, Sir Humphrey, 72–3, 122
Glentaisie, battle of (1565), 123
Gottfried, Rudolf B., 112
Grace, Oliver, 74
Granuaile (Grace O'Malley), 90, 125
Grey de Wilton, Arthur, Lord, 6
Guicciardini, Francesco, 10, 35
Guy, J.A., 112

Hadfield, Andrew, 113
Ham, R.E., 112
Harpoole, Robert, 97, 127
Harrington, Sir Henry, 97–8, 99, 100, 127
Hayes-McCoy, G.A., 116
Heron, Sir Nicholas, 48, 116, 124
Hexter, J.H., 112
Hinton, E.M., 113

Holstein, Adolph, Duke of, 104
Hore, Herbert F., 38, 113
Horsey, Sir Edward, 110
Horsey, William, 56
Howard, L., 112
Howth, Thomas St Lawrence, Lord of, 93

Imokilly, 85
Inchiquin O'Briens, 33

Jenyson, Thomas, 103
Jones, Michael, 112

Kavanaghs, 91
Kerrycurrihy, 70
Kildare, 76
Kildare, Earl of, 16, 55, 94, 120, 126
Kilkenny, 63–4, 76, 78, 97, 99
Killeene, Christopher Plunket, Lord of, 93
Killigrew, Sir Henry, 7, 8
Kilmallock, 50–1, 59, 71, 72, 86
Kinsellas, 92
Knecht, R.J., 112

Lacy, Hugh, 50
Lancaster, Thomas, 60
Laois, 96
Le Strange, Thomas, 74, 89, 116
Leighton, Sir Thomas, 110
Lennon, Colm, 113
Limerick, 18, 51, 71–2, 87
linen act, 78–9
Lixnaw, Baron of, 50, 57
Loughrea, 88
Louth, Lord of, 16, 101
Lynch, John FitzJames, 88

Index

McAuley, 63, 70
MacCann, 55
MacCartan, 44
MacCarthy, Sir Cormock MacTeage, 85
MacCarthy, Sir Dermod MacTeage, 50
MacCarthy More, Donal, *see* Clancare, Earl of
MacCarthy Reagh, 50, 68, 85
MacCoghlans, 76, 84
MacCormac, Cormac, 98, 127
MacDermods, 47
MacDonald, Alistair (Oge MacDonnell), 53, 56, 117
MacDonald, James MacConnell, 83, 107, 123
MacDonald, Sorley Boy (MacDonnell), 82, 83, 117, 123
MacDonoghs, 46, 63, 70
MacGeoghegan, Ross, 57
MacGeoghegans, 84, 107
McGuires, 56, 83
Machiavelli, Niccolo, 35
MacHugh, Feagh, 89, 123
Mackworth, Captain, 100
MacMahon, Art, 101–2
MacMahons, 44
MacMurroughs, 92
MacOliver, Sir John, 125
MacOliver, Shane, 125
MacQuillans, 55, 59, 83, 118
MacRedmonds, 89
MacRorye Reogh, Shane, 98
MacShee, Rory, 72, 122
MacSweenys, 44–5, 85
McTurlough, Callough, 74
McVeagh, John, 113
MacWilliam Burkes, 16, 74, 87, 88, 90, 125

Magennis, 14, 44, 61, 119
Magennis, Sir Hugh, 101, 127
Maguire, Cúchonnacht, 45
Maguire, Séan, 45
Maguires, 44
Malby, Sir Nicholas, 33, 47, 56, 63, 91, 100, 109, 114, 116, 125
Marshall (soldier), 65
Mary, Queen of Scots, 5
Mary I, Queen of England, 4, 128
Masterton, Thomas, 33, 91, 92, 125
Molyneaux, Edmund, 109, 128
Monasterevin, 109
Monluc, Blaise de Lasseran-Mussencome, seigneur de, 10–11
Morgan, Hiriam, 118, 128
Mullaghmast massacre (1581), 34
Mulryne, J.R., 112

Netterville, Richard, 95, 126
Newry, 98–9
Nicholls, Kenneth, 112, 115
Norris, Sir Henry, 80
Norris, Sir John, 82, 123
Northumberland, John Dudley, Duke of, 4, 116, 128
Nugent, Christopher, 92–3, 126
Nugent, Nicholas, 93, 96, 126

O'Boyles, 44
O'Brien, Conor, *see* Earl of Thomond
O'Brien, Donough, 87, 124
O'Brien, Mahon, 87, 124
O'Brien, Teige MacConor, 75, 122
O'Brien, Teige MacMurrough, 75, 122
O'Briens, 47
O'Byrne, Hugh MacShane, 77, 123
O'Byrnes, 92, 126, 127

O'Carrolls, 57, 76, 84
O'Connor, Cormac, 98, 127
O'Connor Dun, 47
O'Connor Ro, 47
O'Connor Sligo, 57, 88
Octavia (play), 9
O'Dohertys, 44
O'Donnell, Callough (Calvagh), 44, 45, 46, 56, 115, 119
O'Donnell, Conn, 56, 119
O'Donnell, Sir Hugh, 14–15, 21, 30, 31, 33, 46, 48, 88, 116, 119
O'Donnellys, 55
O'Dowds, 46
O'Dwyers, 84
O'Farrells, 47, 116
Offaly, 97
O'Flannigans, 47
O'Flynns, 47
O'Gallaghers, 44
O'Hanlons, 44
O'Haras, 46
O'Kanes, 55
O'Keeffes, 63, 70
O'Kellys, 47, 116
Ó Laidhin, Tomás, 113
O'Maddens, 47
O'Maghers, 84
O'Malley, Grace (Granuaile), 90, 125
O'Molloy, Callogh, 108
O'Molloys, 84, 107–8
O'More, Cahir, 76, 123
O'More, Kedagh (Cadogh), 76, 123
O'More, Lysagh, 76, 123
O'More, Rory Oge, 34–5, 96–8, 100–1, 109, 126–7
O'Mores, 96, 107
O'Neill, Brian MacFelim, 119

O'Neill, Conn Bacach, 115, 118
O'Neill, Felim Caoch, 118
O'Neill, Hugh, 54, 55–6, 118
O'Neill, Shane, 13, 14, 21, 23, 24, 25, 30, 34, 44–9, 56, 58, 78, 115
  death of, 53–4
O'Neill, Turlough Brasselagh, 55, 118
O'Neill, Turlough Luineach, 15, 30, 31, 56, 59, 67, 75, 82, 83, 98–9, 118, 119
  submission of, 54–5, 109
O'Quinns, 55
O'Reilly, John, 57
Ormond, Thomas Butler, tenth Earl of, 16, 23–5, 28, 29, 30, 34, 49–50, 53, 57, 62, 70, 71–2, 74, 75, 80–1, 97, 100, 117
O'Rourkes, 46
Osborne, James M., 113
O'Shaughnessys, 87, 124–5
Ossary, Baron of Upper (Sir Barnaby FitzPatrick), 14, 33, 34, 64, 76, 93, 100–1, 120
O'Sullivan Bere, 63, 70
O'Sullivan More, 63, 70
O'Tooles, 92, 126, 127
oyer and *terminer* (judicial commissions), 91, 100

Pale, opposition to composition tax, 17, 19, 22–3, 92–6, 126
Parker, John, 98
Pelham, Lord, 114
Perrot, Sir John, 19, 73, 122, 123
Piers, William, 33, 53, 56, 75, 77, 118
Plunket, Christopher, 93
Power, Anthony, 65
Power, Richard Lord, 71, 84, 122

Index

Quinn, D.B., 113, 128

Radcliffe, Thomas, *see* Sussex, Earl of
Raleigh, Sir Walter, 114
Randolph, Colonel Edward, 45, 48
Rathlin Island, 82, 107
Reynolds, 46
Ribner, Irving, 115
Roche, David, first Viscount, 16, 50, 68, 85, 86, 124
Roche, James, 70
Rokeby, Ralph, 74, 122
Roscommon, 47, 116
Russell Major, J., 115

St Lawrence, Thomas, 93
St Leger, Sir Anthony, 28
St Leger, Lady Ursula, 64, 120
St Leger, Sir Warham, 48, 49, 52, 58, 114, 116, 121
Sanders, Nicholas, 16
Savage, Lord, 55
Scurlock, Barnaby, 95, 126
Sherlock, Patrick, 74, 122
Shewring, Margaret, 112
Shrule Castle, 74
Sidney, Sir Henry
  career, 4–6
    first term, 5, 44–59
    second term, 5, 59–81, 112
    third term, 5, 81–103
    in Wales, 5, 6, 103–4, 105
  colonising policies, 13–14, 15–16, 18–19, 33–4
  composition tax, 17, 19–20, 22–3, 32–3, 92–6, 126
  coyne and livery, 28–9, 62
  establishes provincial councils, 18–19
  finances, 43–4, 103, 104–5, 106, 108, 115
  memoirs
    aims in writing, 1–4, 5–7, 12, 23, 36
    comparisons, 7–12, 35
    compatibility with events, 21–3, 26, 108
    drafts of, 1–4
    interpretations of, 12–13, 16, 17, 18, 36
    length of, 8
    manuscript copies, 38
    self-justification in, 23, 94–5, 102–3, 104, 106
    style of, 8–9, 20
    topical selectivity of, 5–6, 12, 18–19, 20
  military garrisons, 33–4, 82–3, 90–1
  oyer and *terminer* (judicial commissions), 91, 100
  parliamentary role, 21–2, 78–80
  political analysis, 28–31, 35–6
  and religious issues, 17–18, 86
  revenue collecting, 32, 35–6
  and Rory Oge O'More, 34–5, 96–8, 100–1, 109
  settlement with chieftains, 54–9
  and Shane O'Neill, 21, 44–9, 53–4, 58
  submission of Turlough Luineach O'Neill, 54–7, 109
  superior attitude of, 14, 15
  youth, 106
Sidney, Lady Mary (*nee* Dudley), 10, 48, 53, 105, 116, 121
Sidney, Sir Philip, 1, 10, 11, 35, 43, 90, 97, 109, 111, 114

Sidney, Robert, 115
Skeffington, Sir William, 128
Slane, James Fleming, Lord of, 93
Sligo, 46–7
Smith, Sir Thomas, 13, 110, 128
Spencer, T.J.B., 112
Stone, Lawrence, 115
Stukely, Thomas, 73, 122
Sussex, Thomas Radcliffe, third Earl of, 28–9, 58, 107, 114, 128
Sute, Captain John, 64, 72
Swords, 78–9
Synott, Richard, 92

taxes, 32, 35–6
   composition, 17, 19–20, 22–3, 32–3, 92–6, 126
   coyne and livery, 28–9, 62
   on wine, 79
Thomond, Conor O'Brien, third Earl of, 15, 30, 52, 63, 73–5, 80, 87, 117
Tipperary, 64–6, 78
Treadwell, Victor, 114
Tremayne, Edmund, 19, 35, 65, 120
Trimbleston, Patrick Barnewall, Lord of, 93

Ulster Journal of Archeology, 38, 113

Van Dorster, Jan, 114
Vaughan, James, 56
Vaughan, Thomas, 54

Wales, Sidney in, 5, 6, 103–4, 105
Wallace, M.W., 111, 115
Walsingham, Sir Francis, 1, 4, 11, 43
Ward, Captain John, 64, 72
Warwick, John, Earl of, 106
Waterford, 65, 67, 71, 84
Waterhouse, Sir Edward, 100, 109, 127
Wexford, 62, 76, 88–9, 92
White, Nicholas, 52
White Knight (Thomas FitzGibbon), 68, 69, 70, 78, 121
Williams, Penry, 111
Woodford, Robert, 94
Worcester, John Tiptoft, Earl of, 61, 120
Worden, Blair, 115
Wyse, John, 65